BUTTERFLY COLORING BOOK

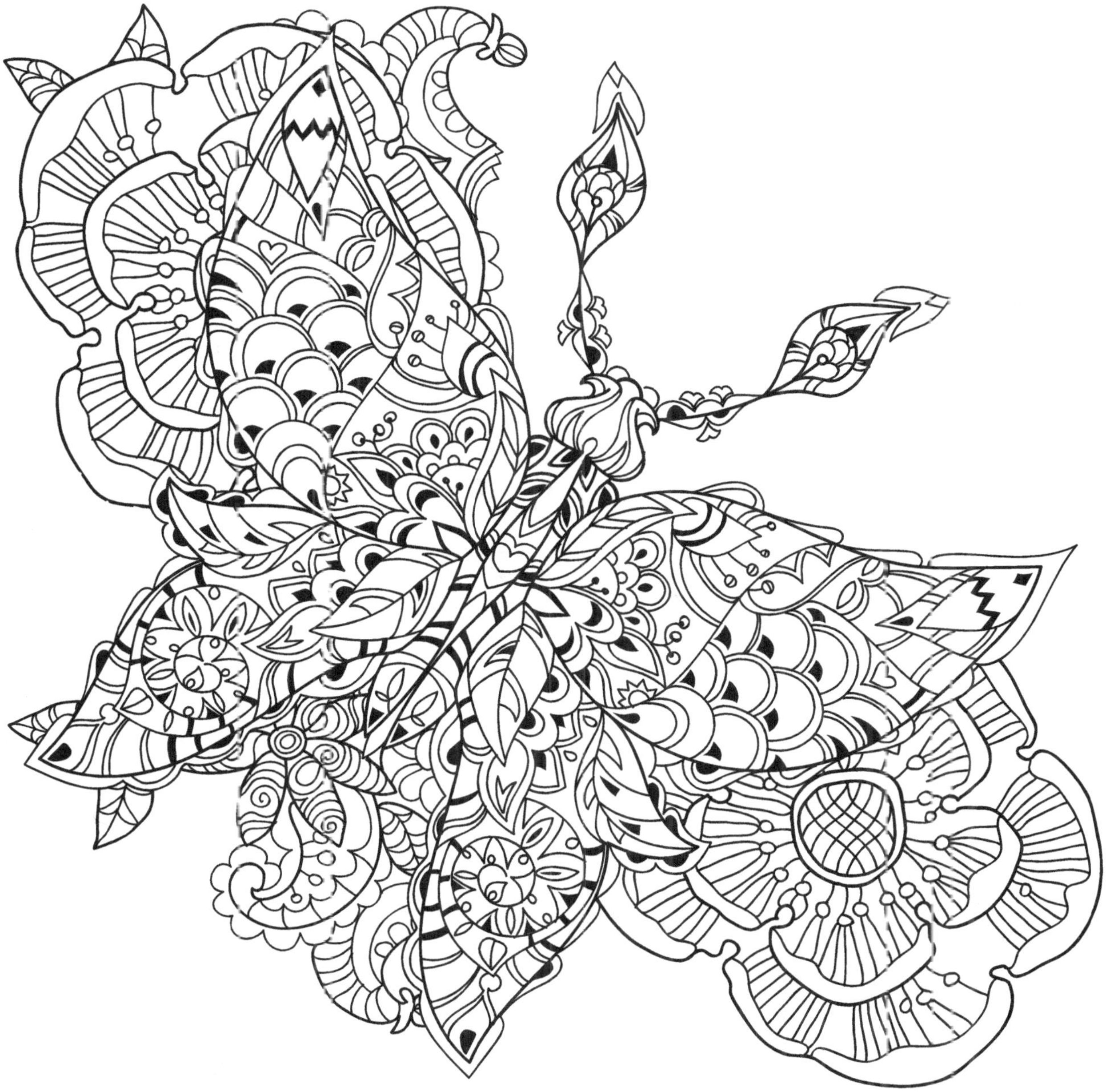

– RUSS FOCUS –

ISBN-13: 978-1727088816 ISBN-10: 1727088816
PUBLISHED BY RUSS FOCUS

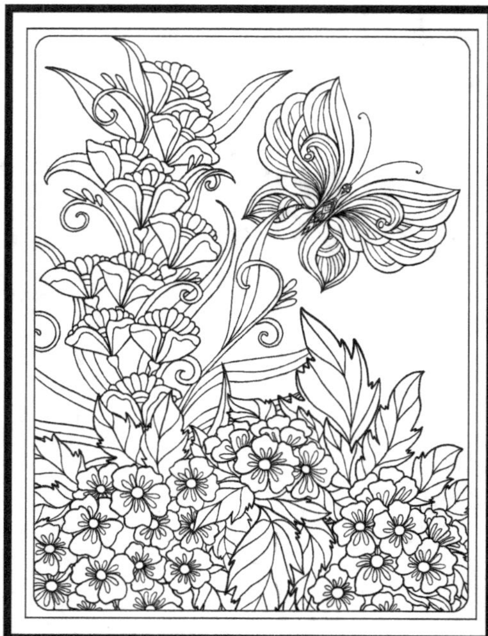

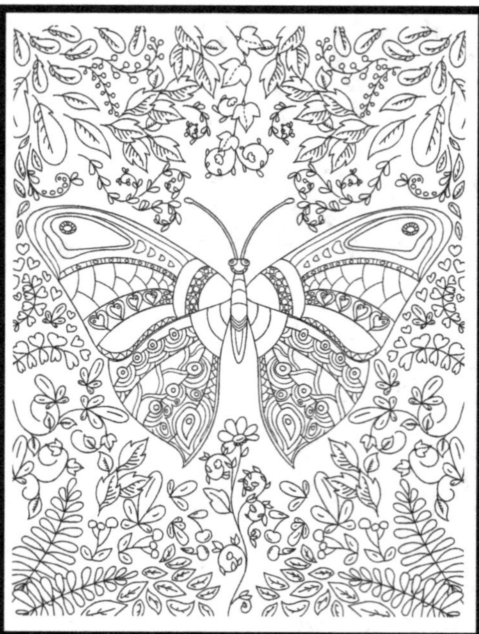

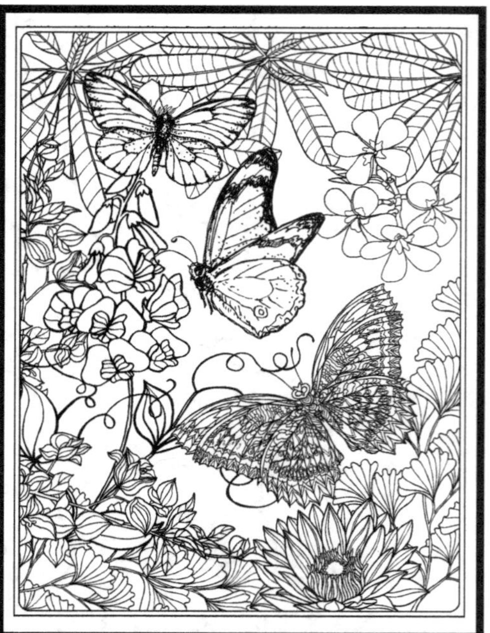

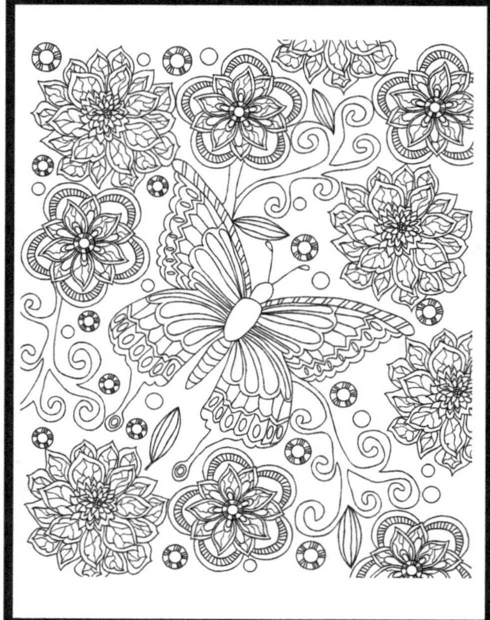

SAMPLE
BUTTERFLY
COLORING
17 of 47
PAGES

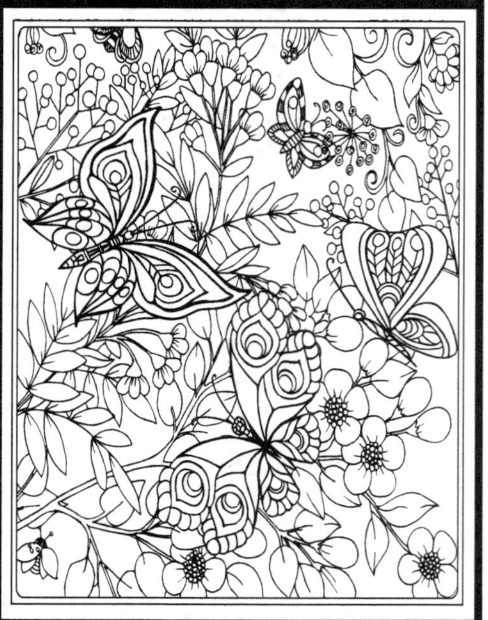

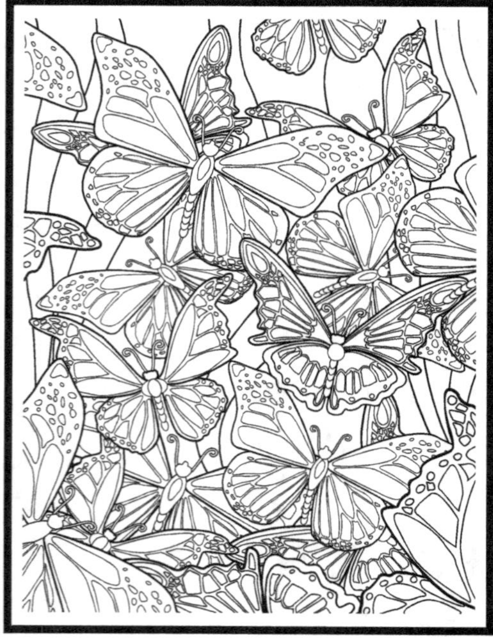

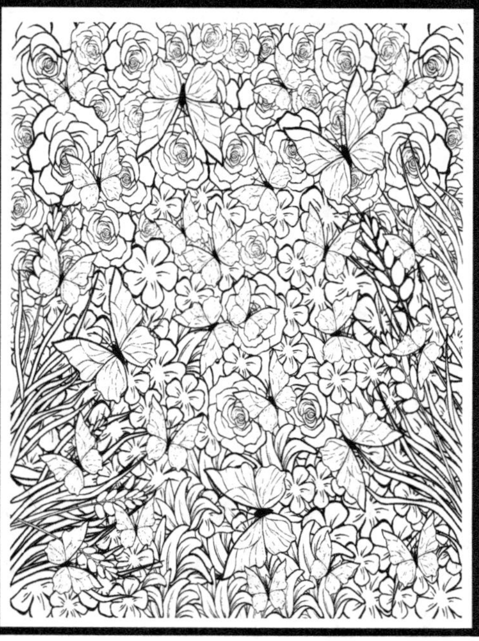

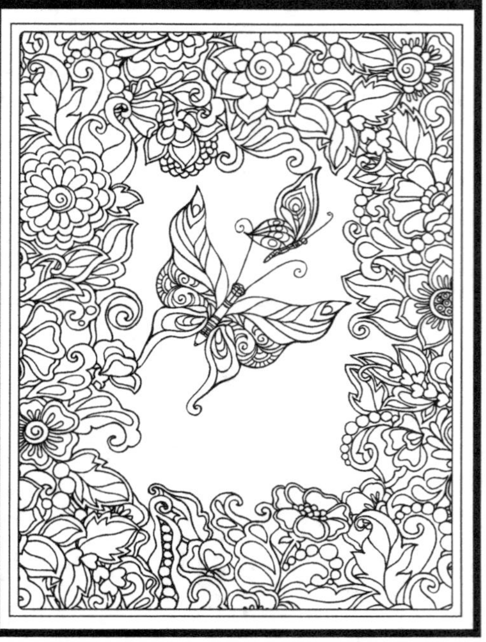

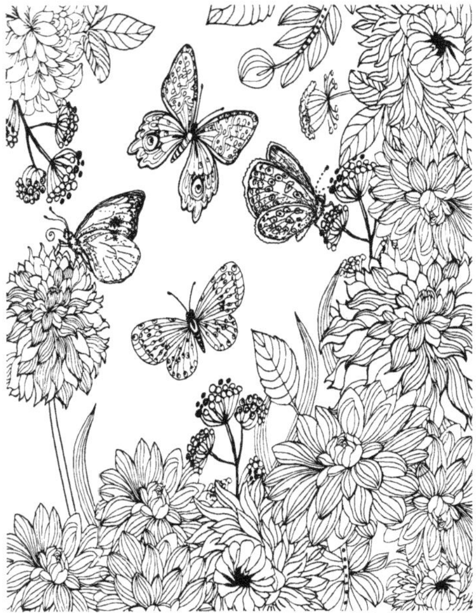
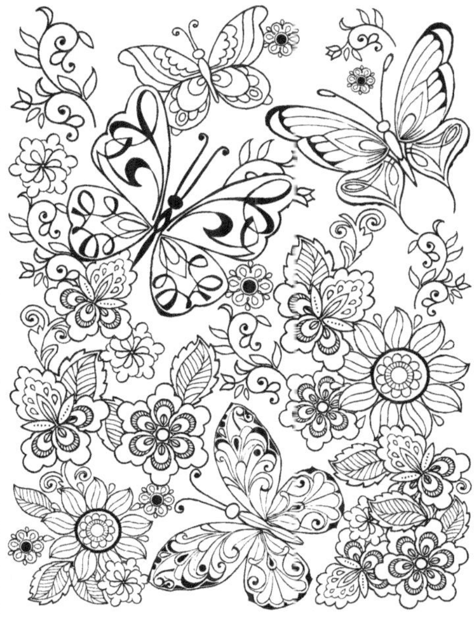
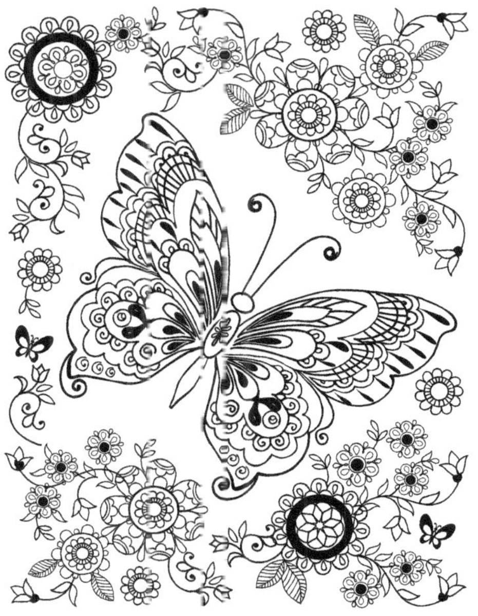
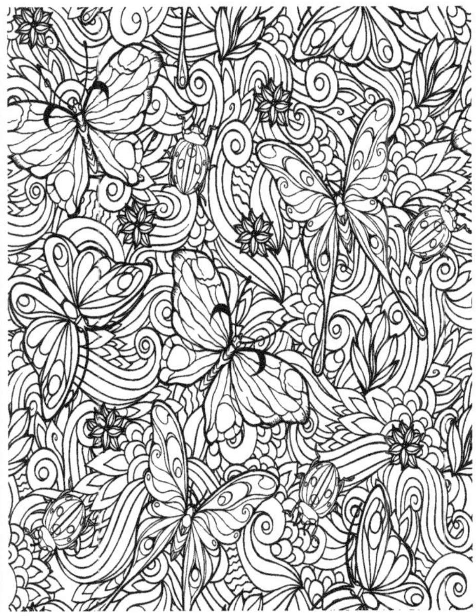
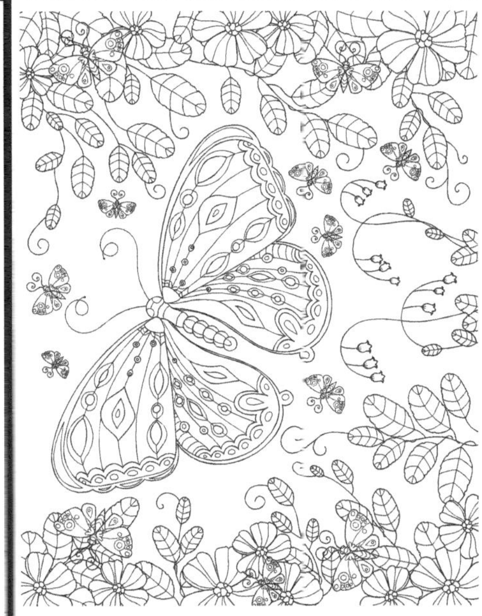
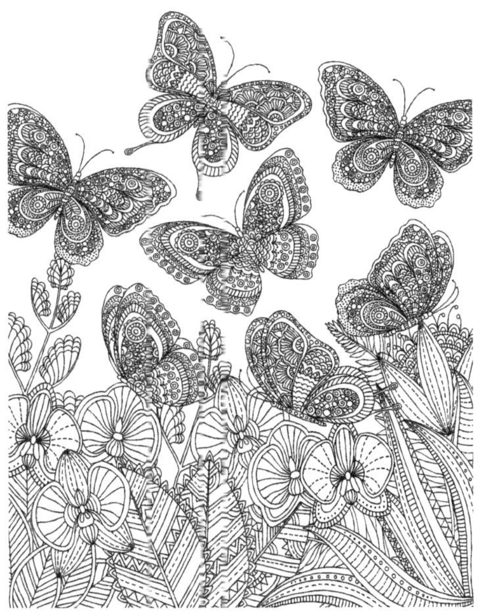
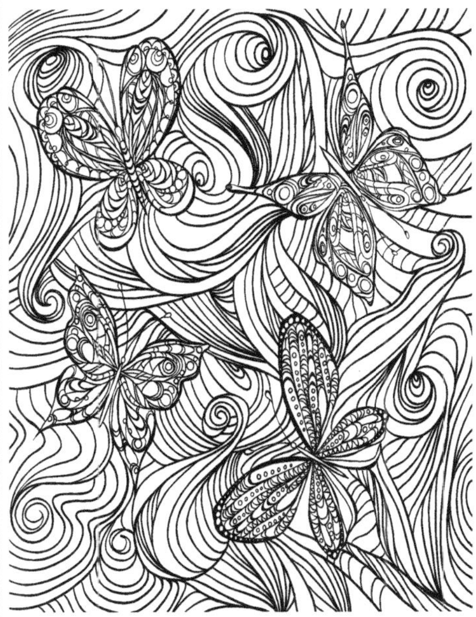
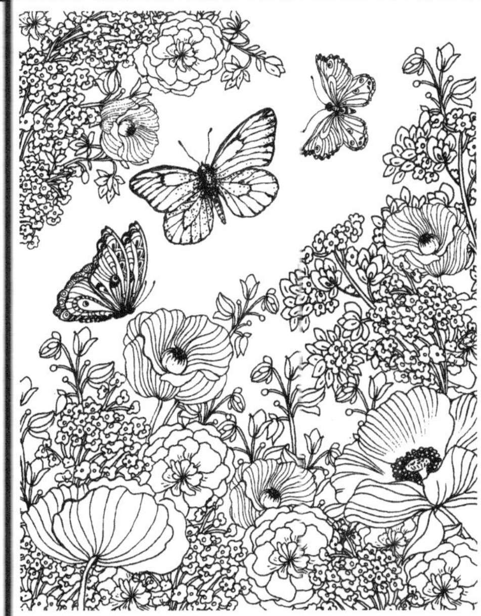
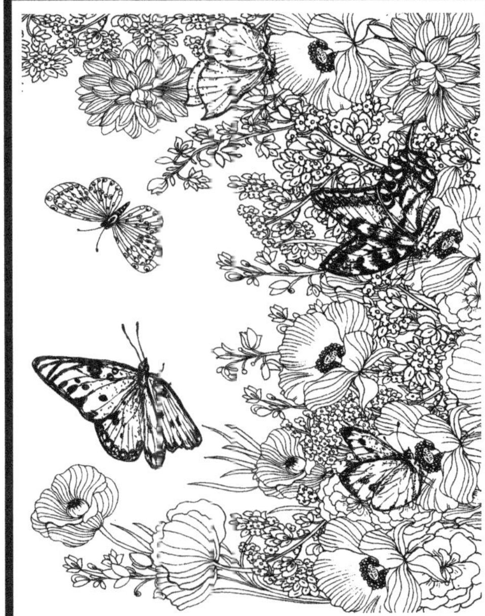

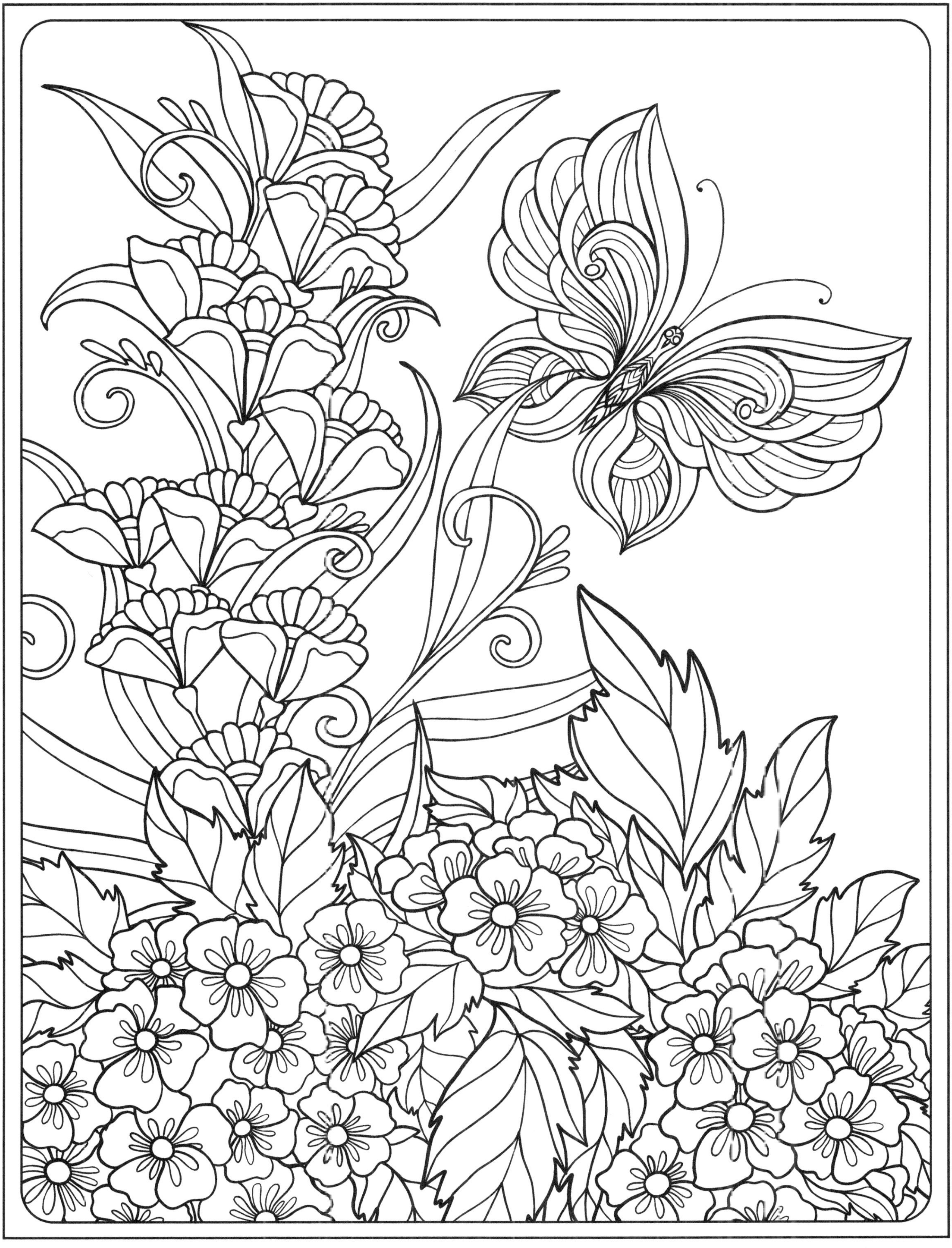

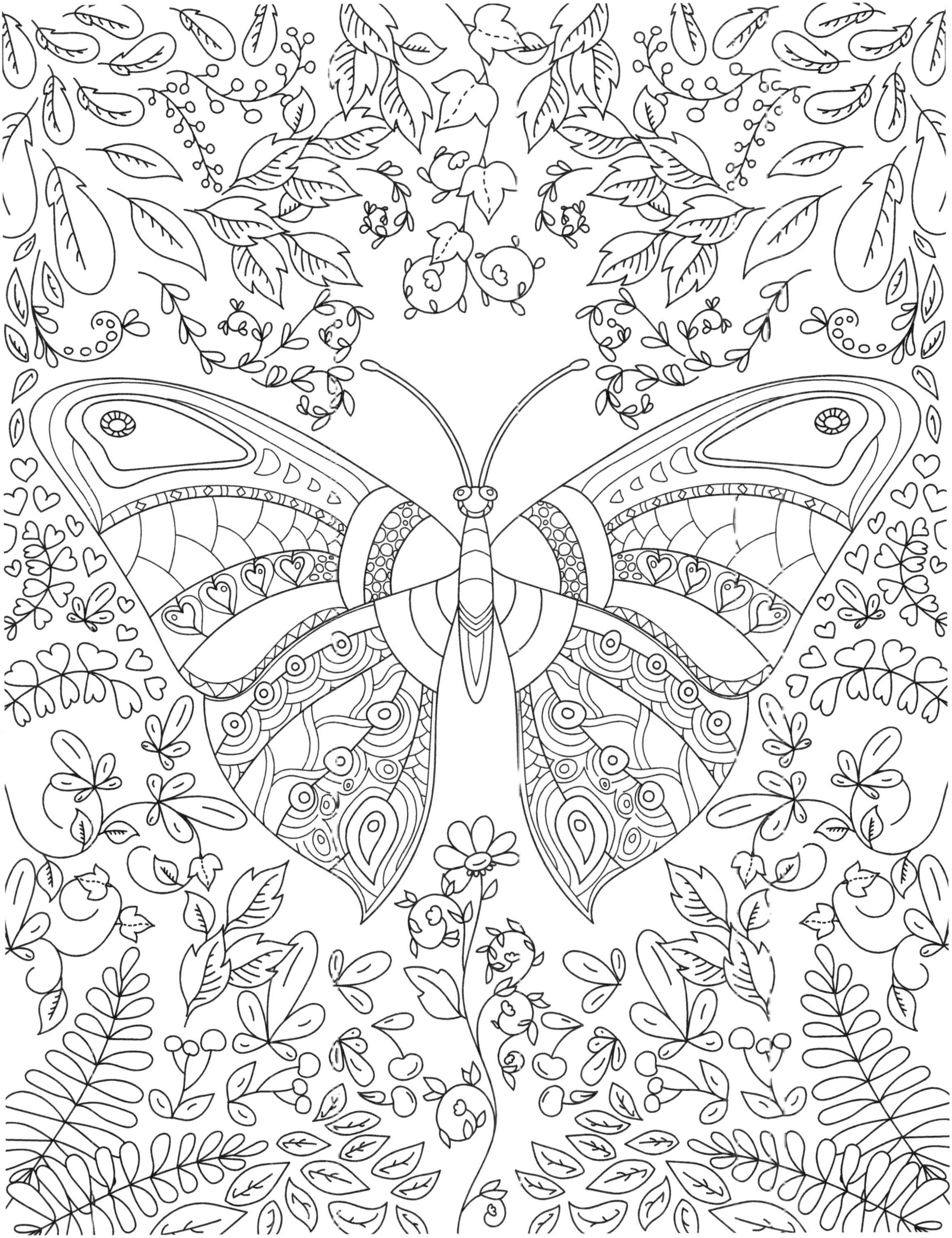

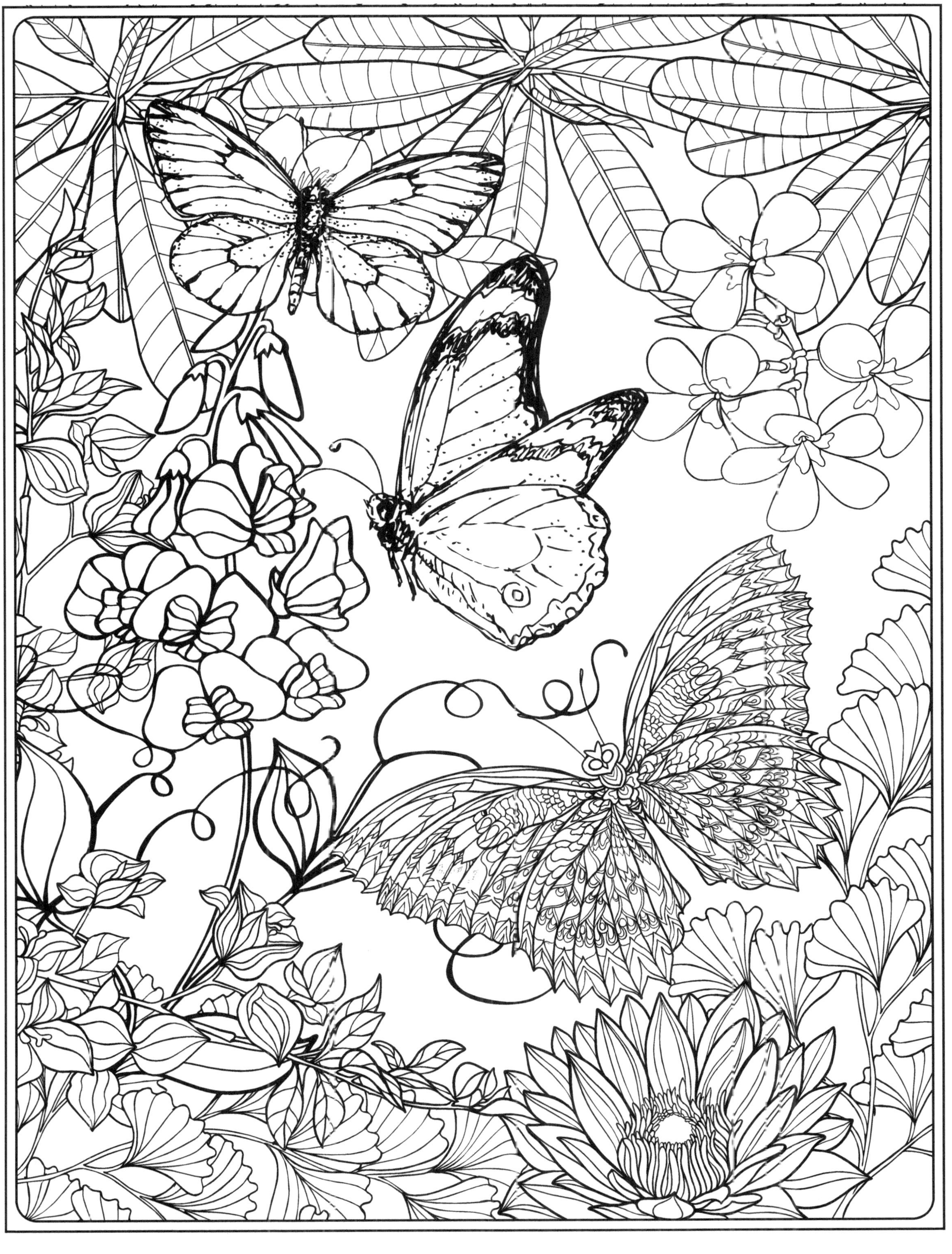

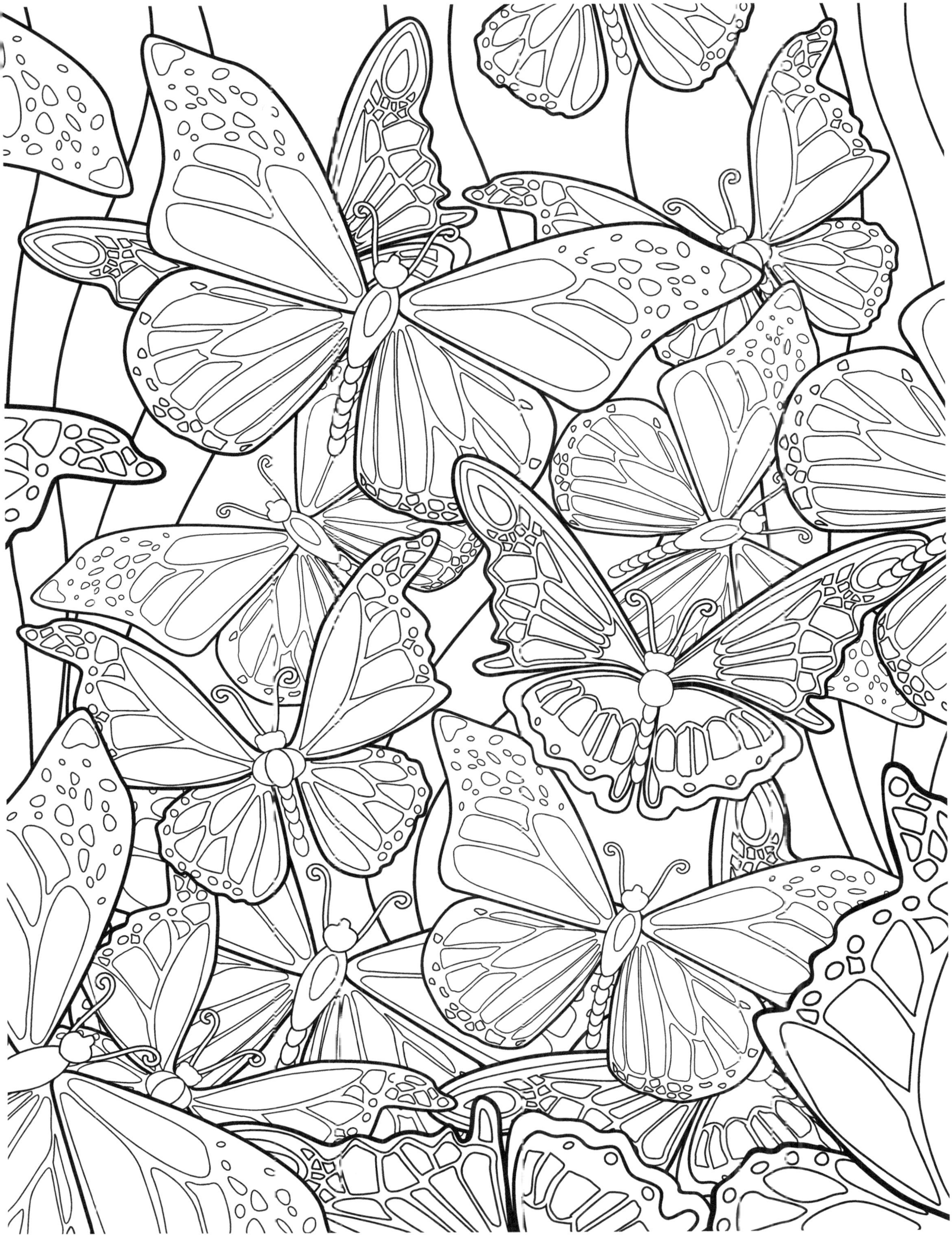

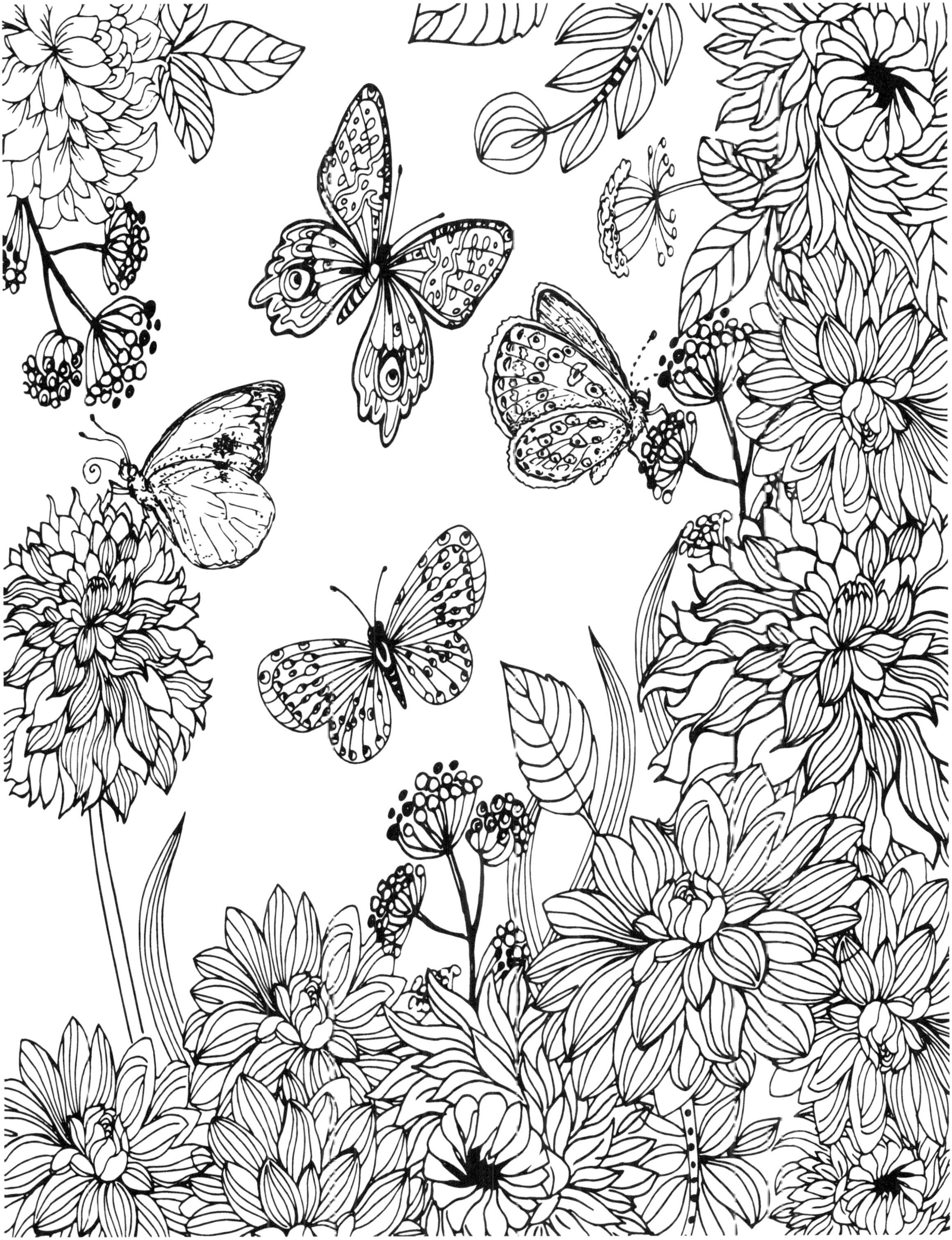

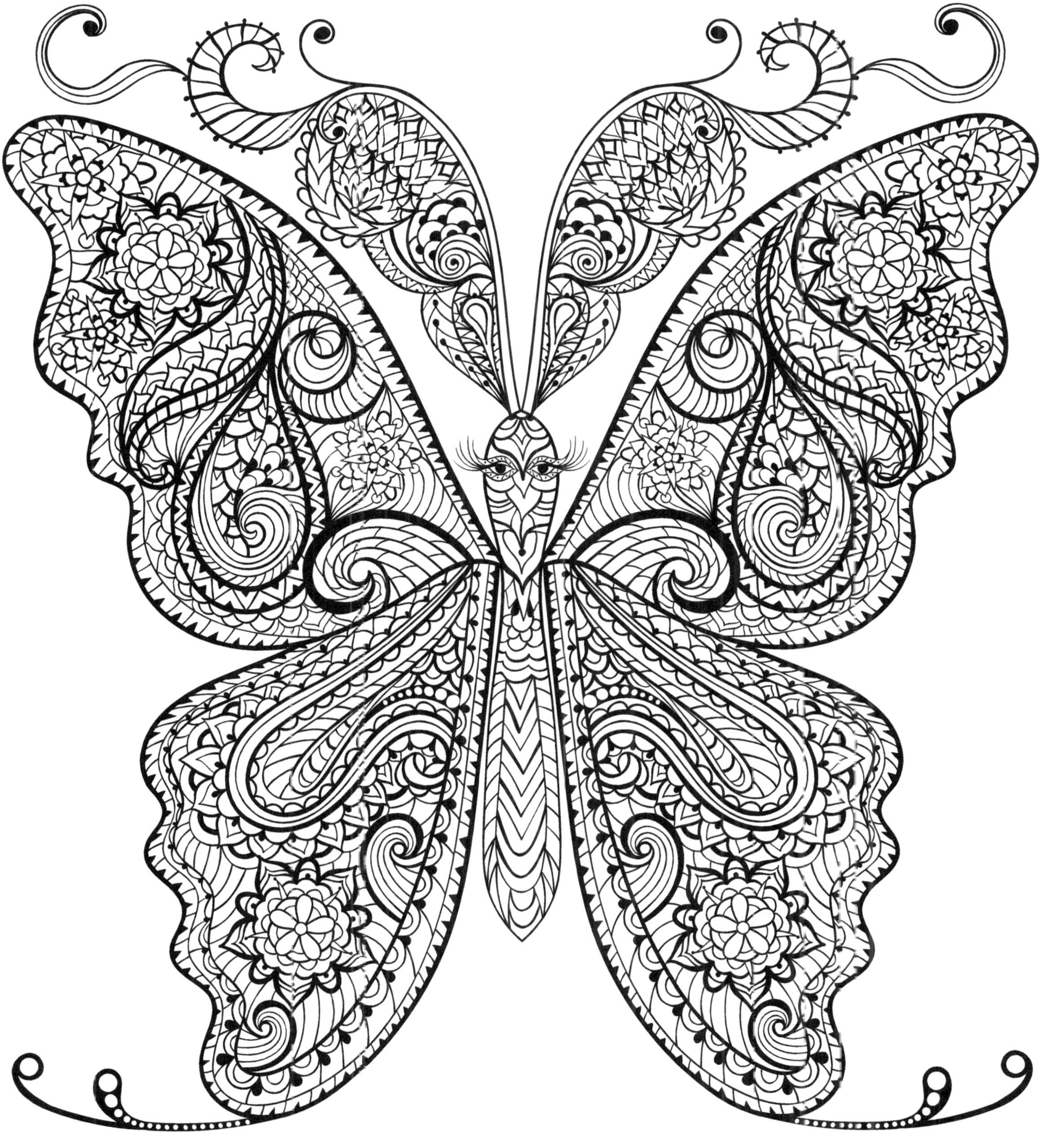

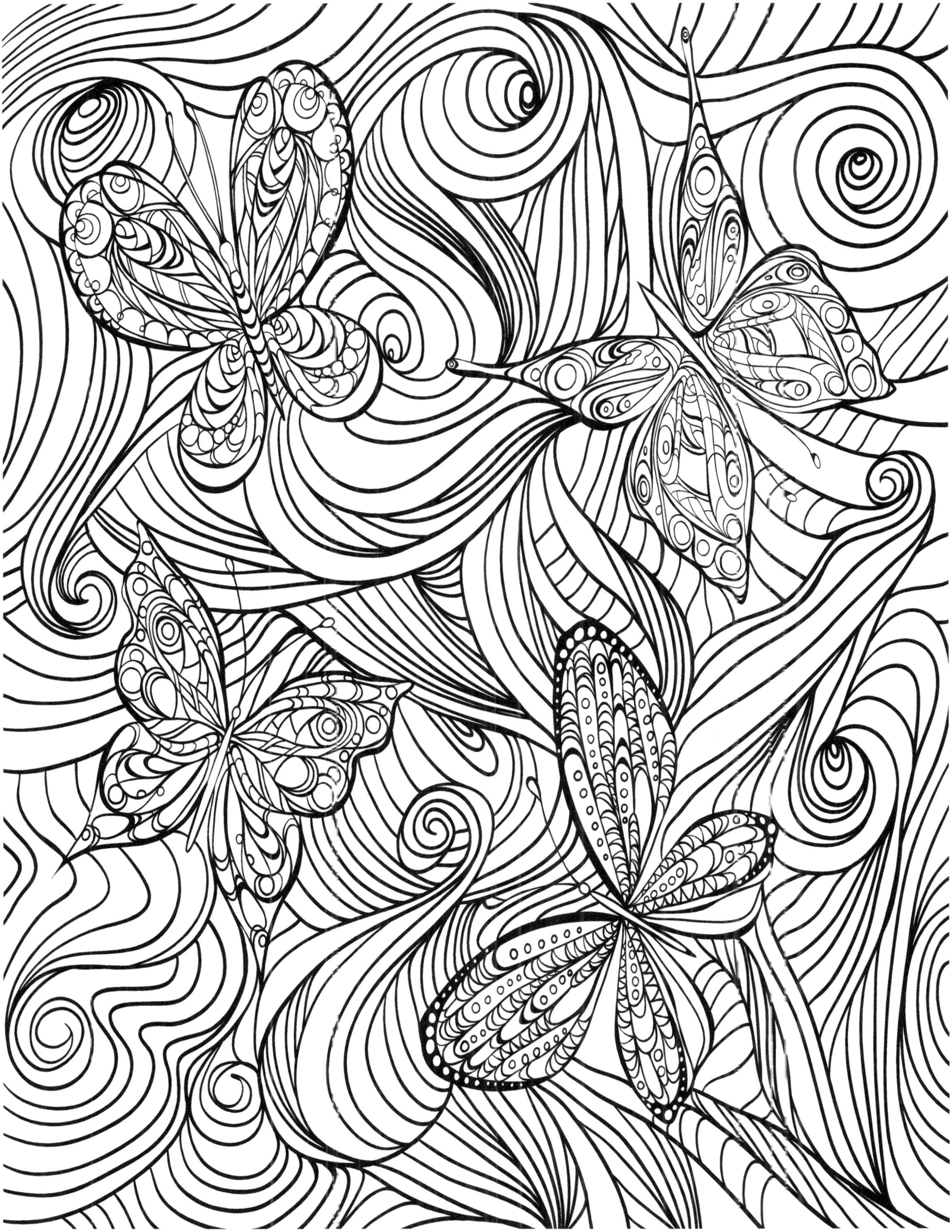

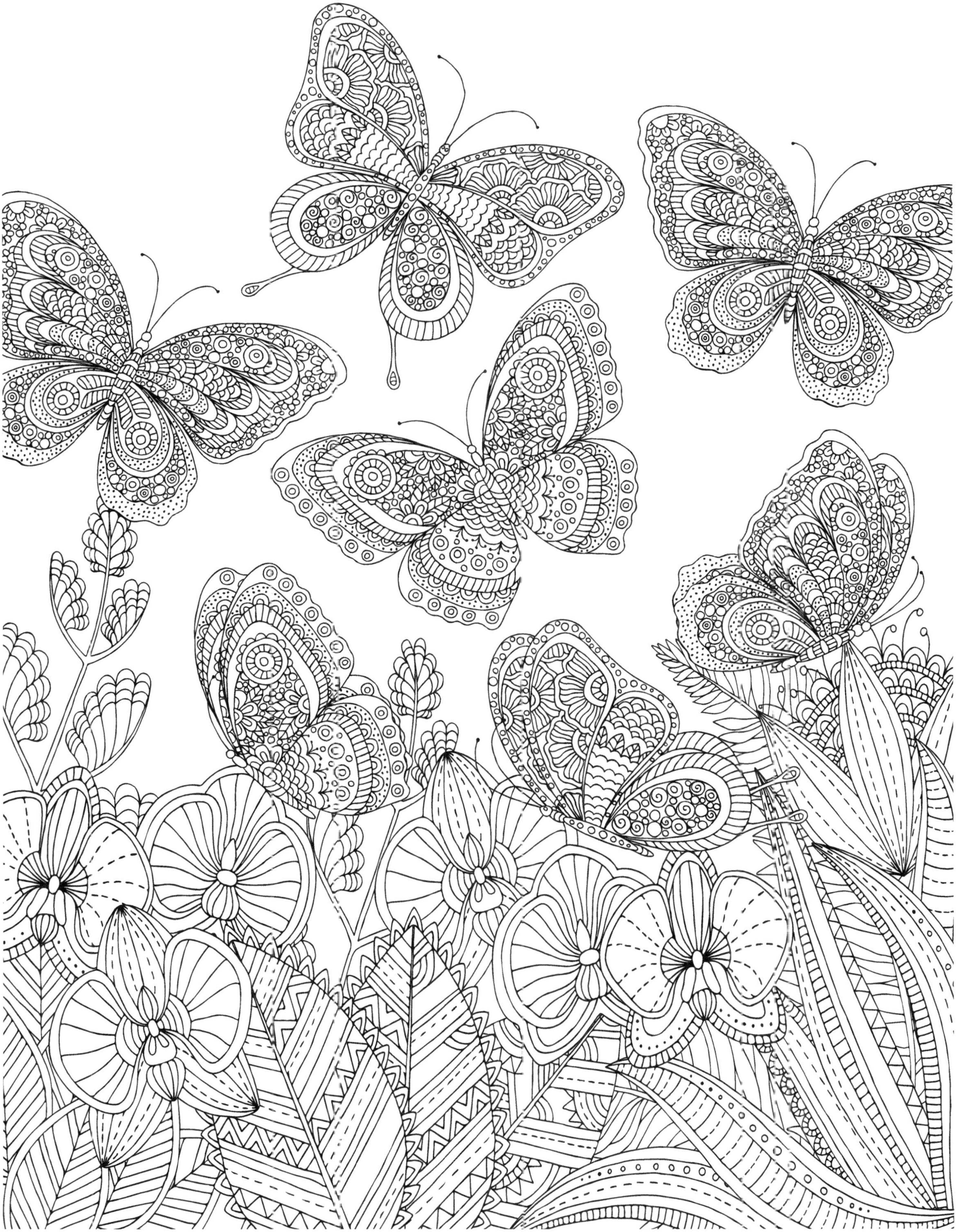

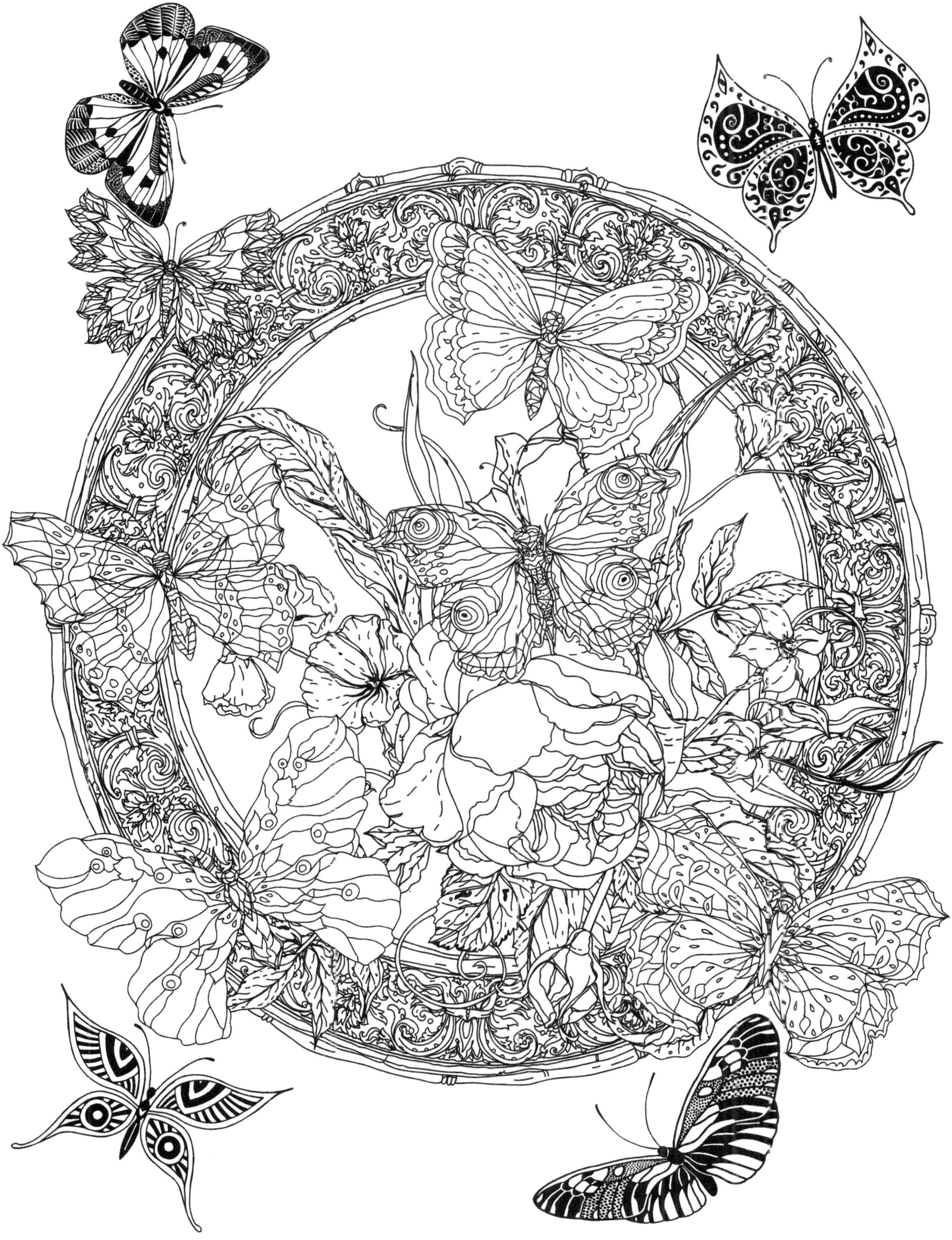

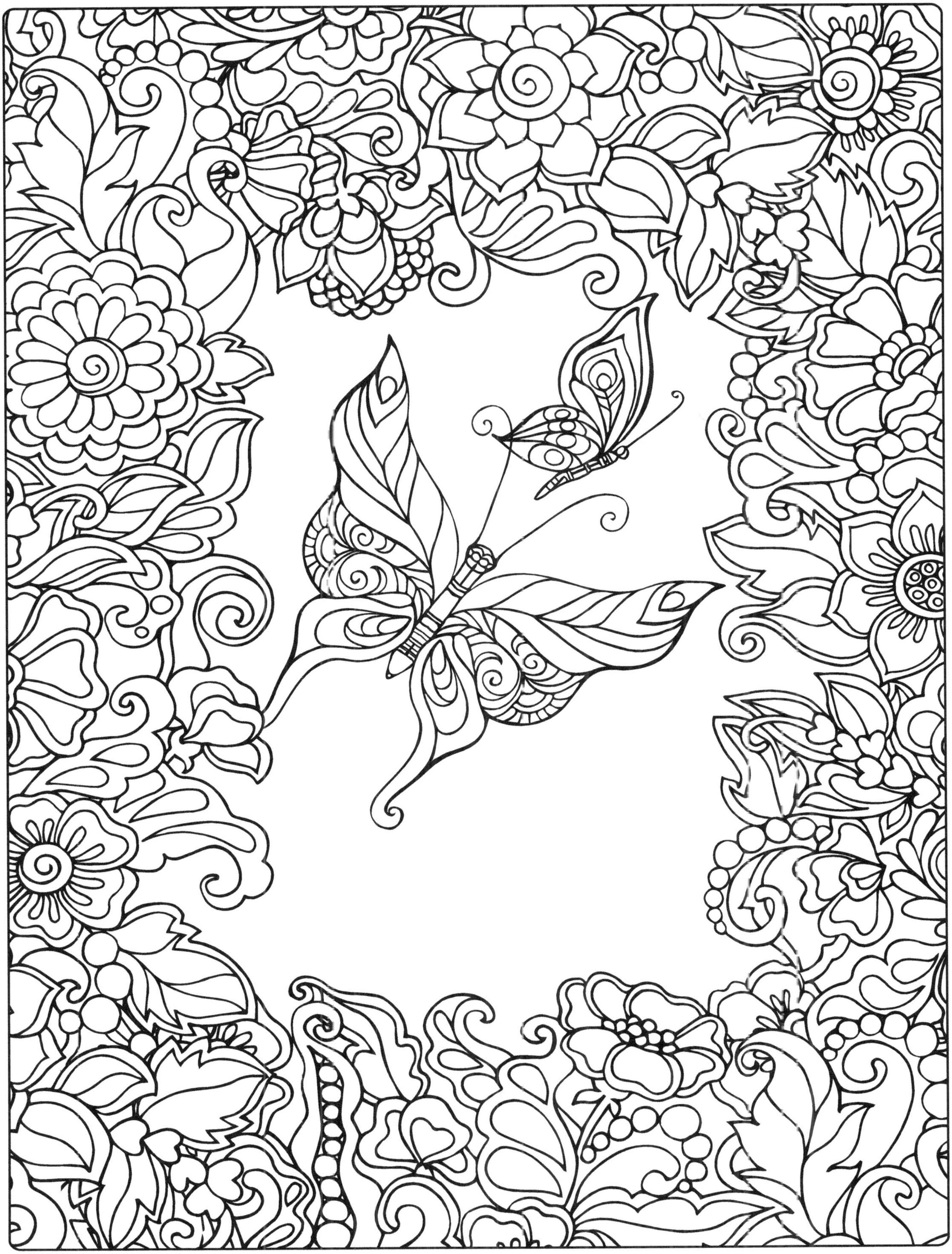

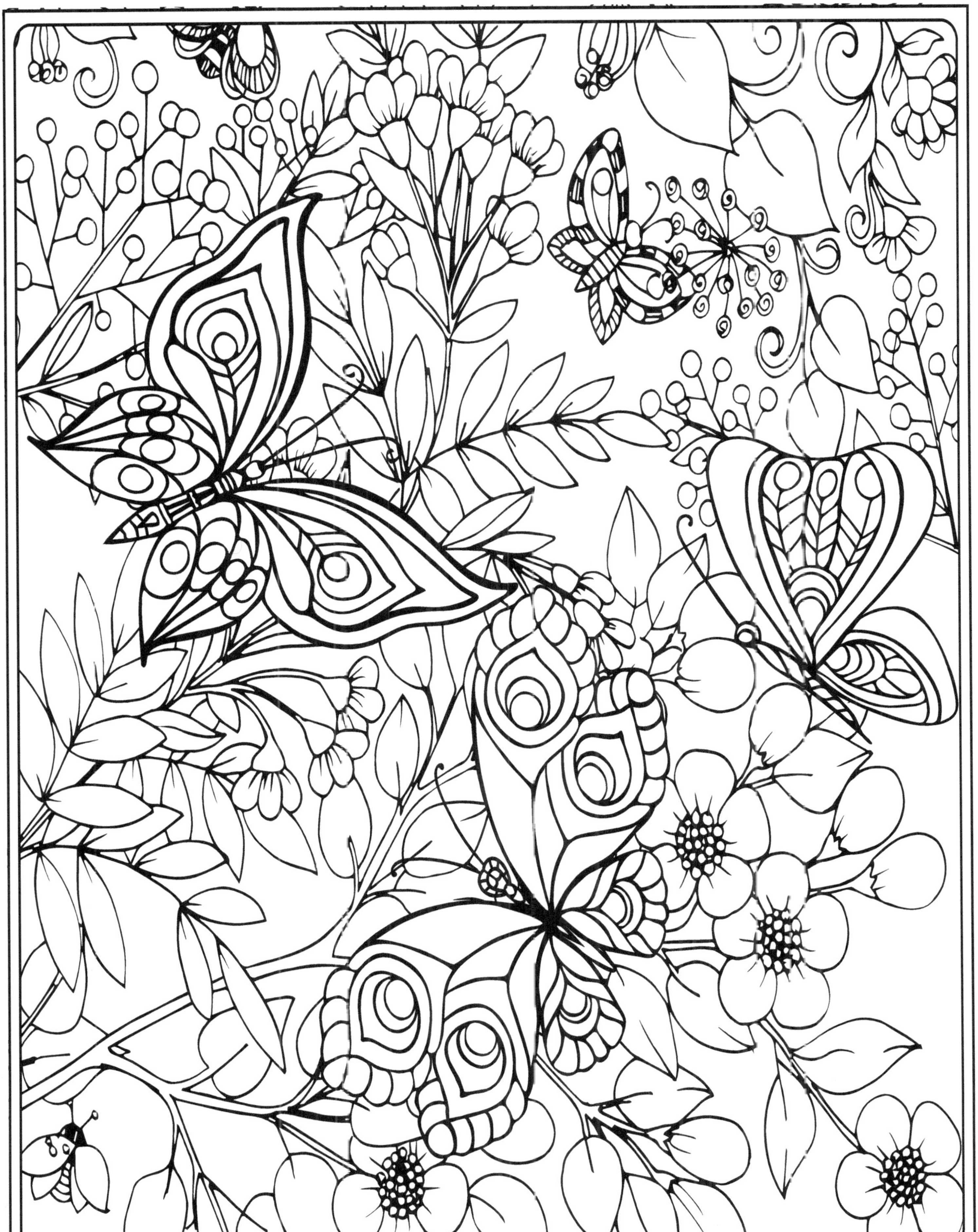

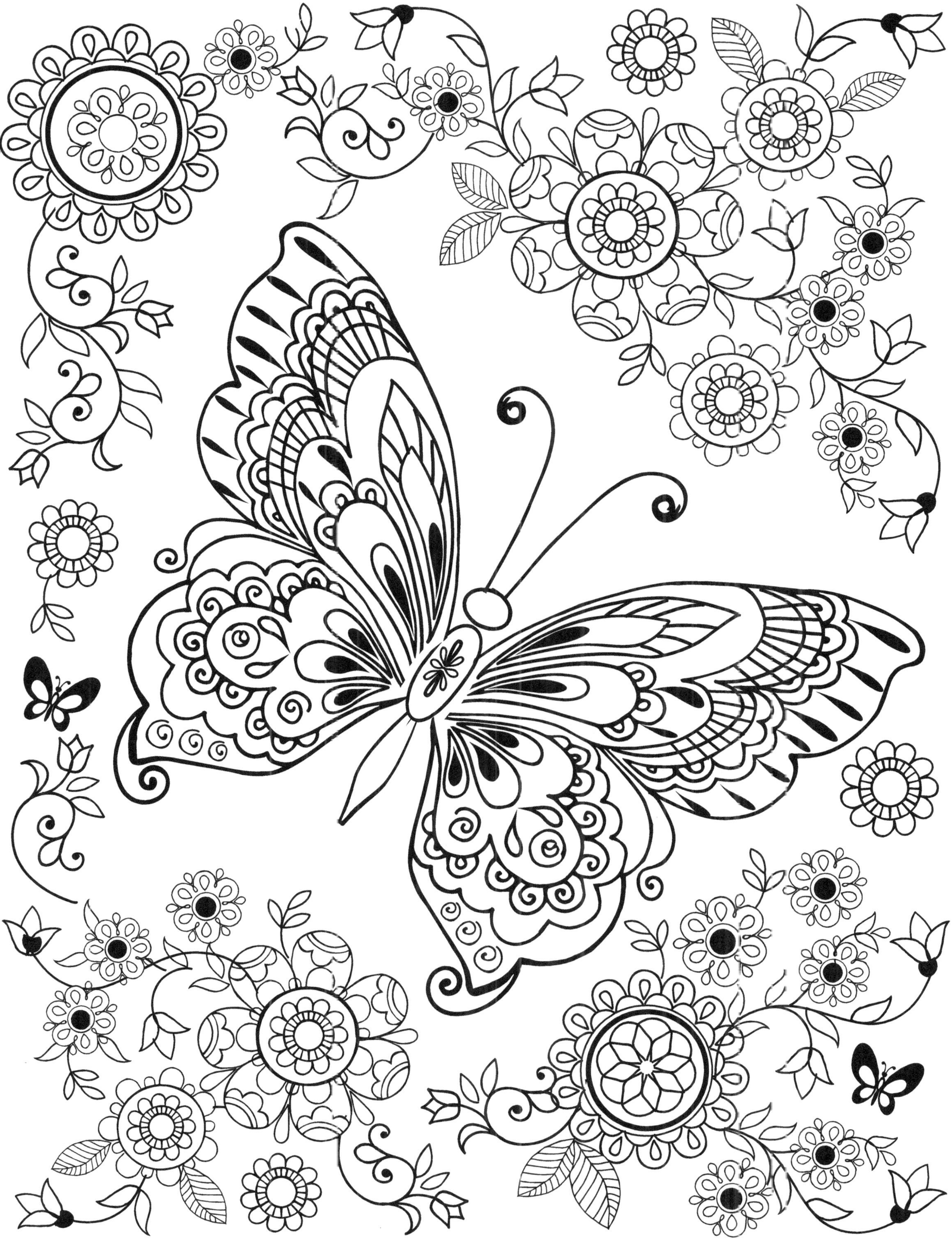

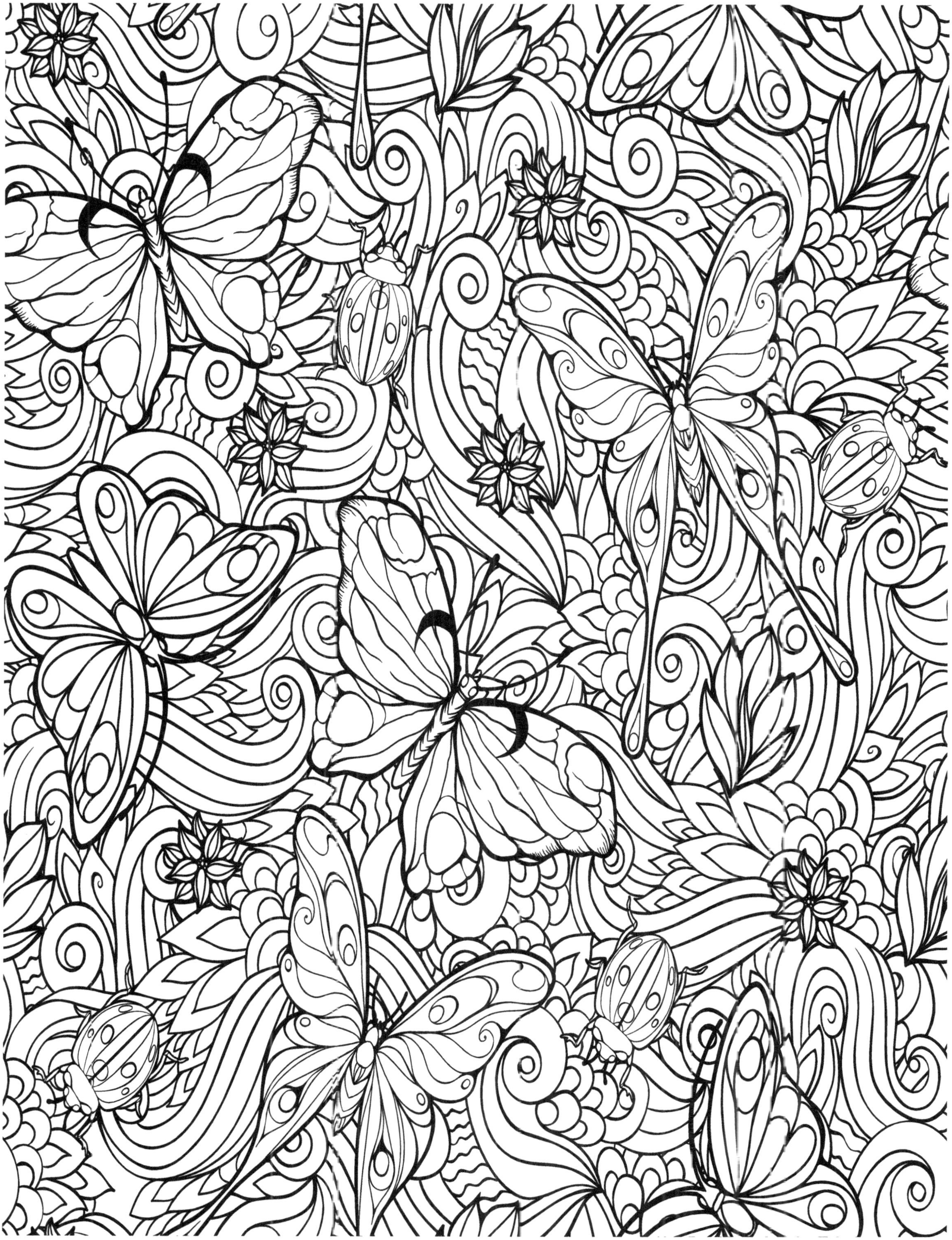

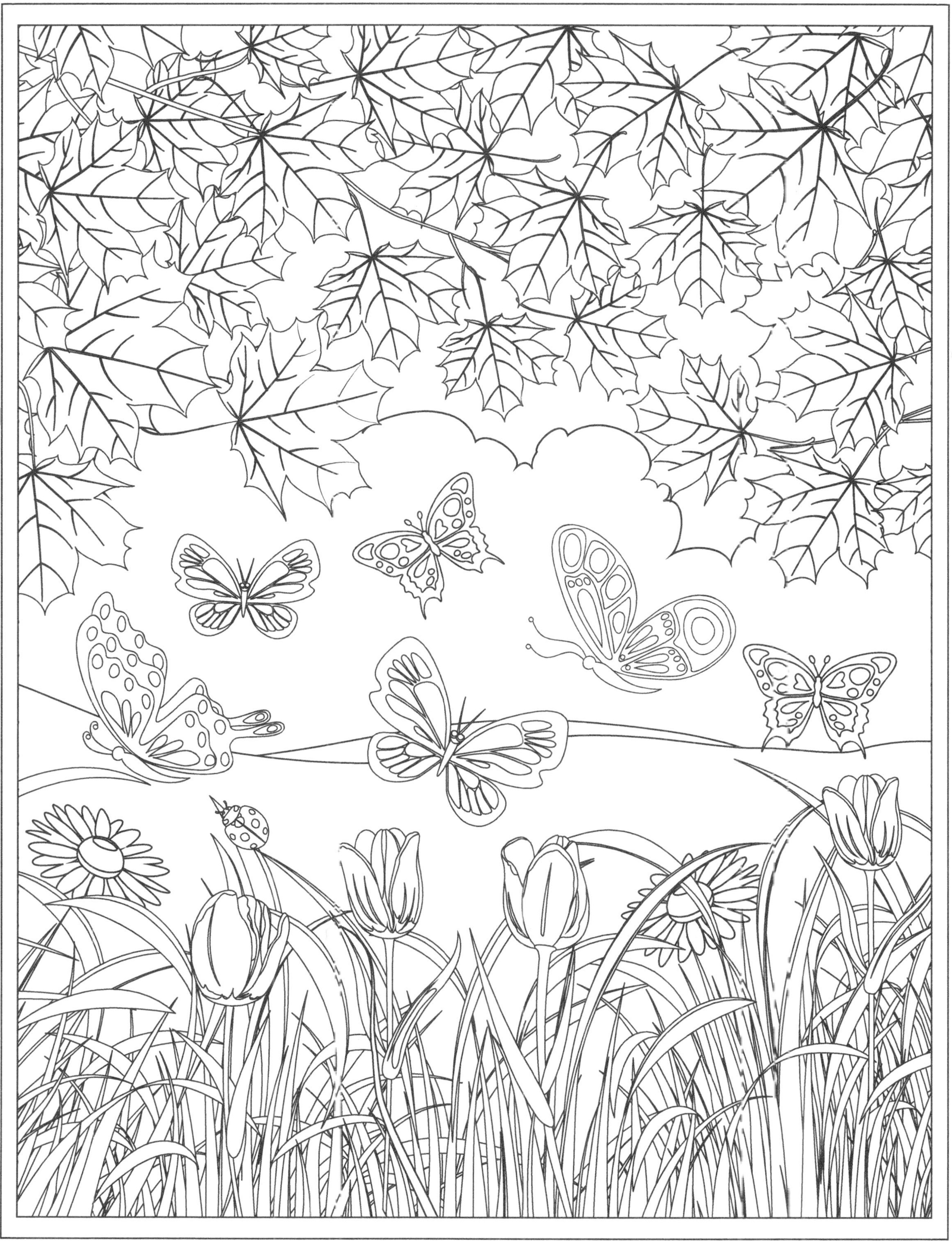

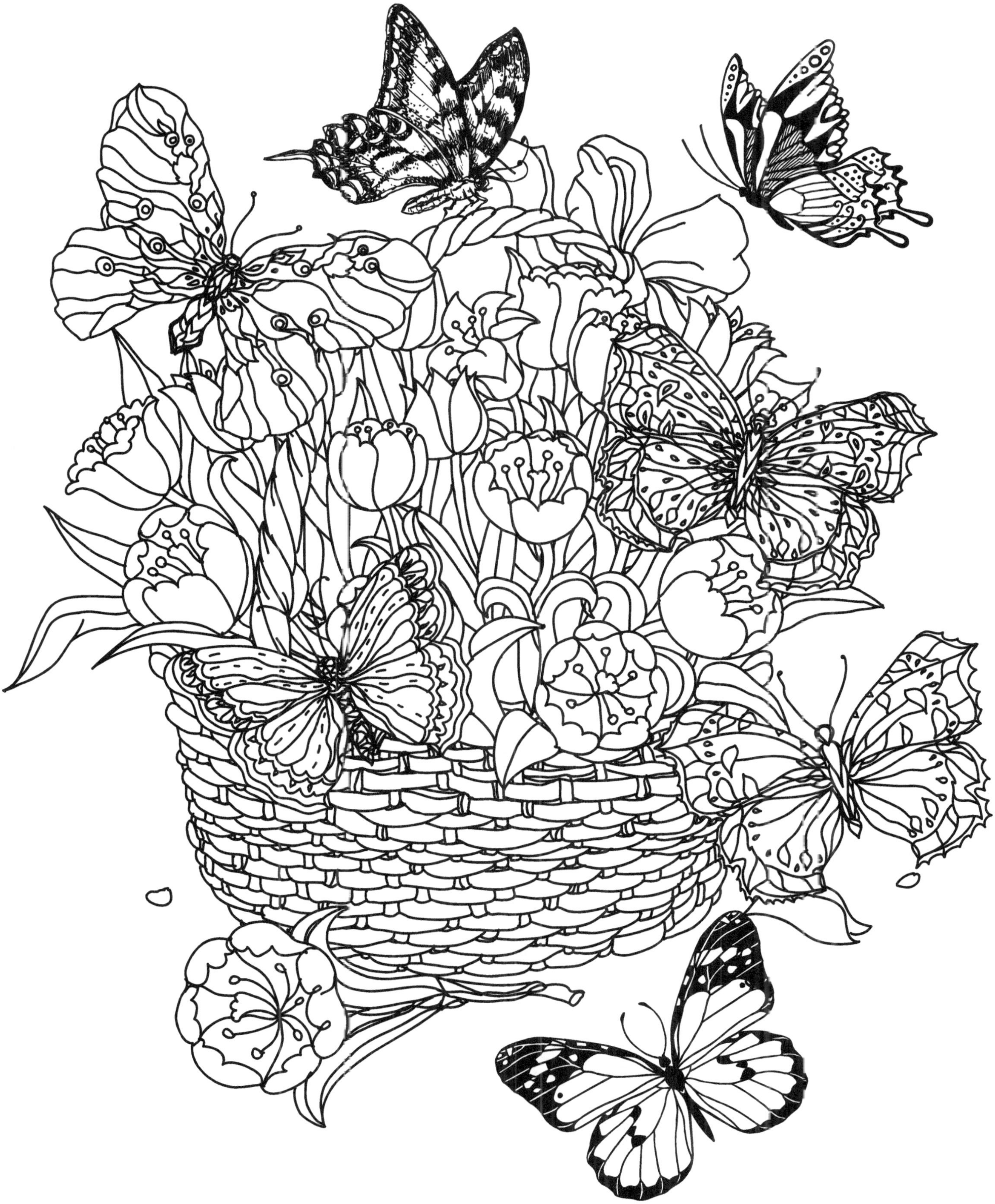

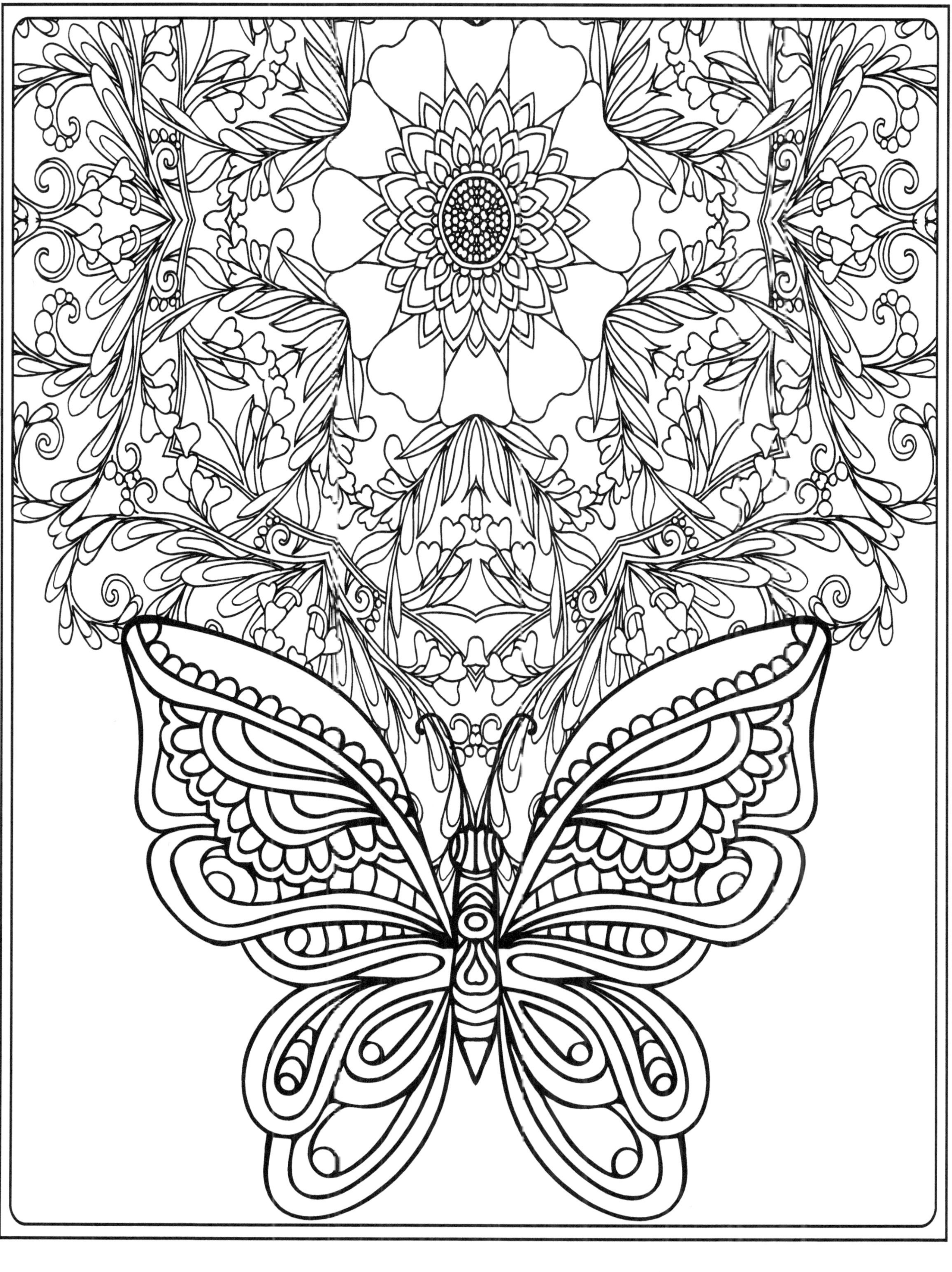

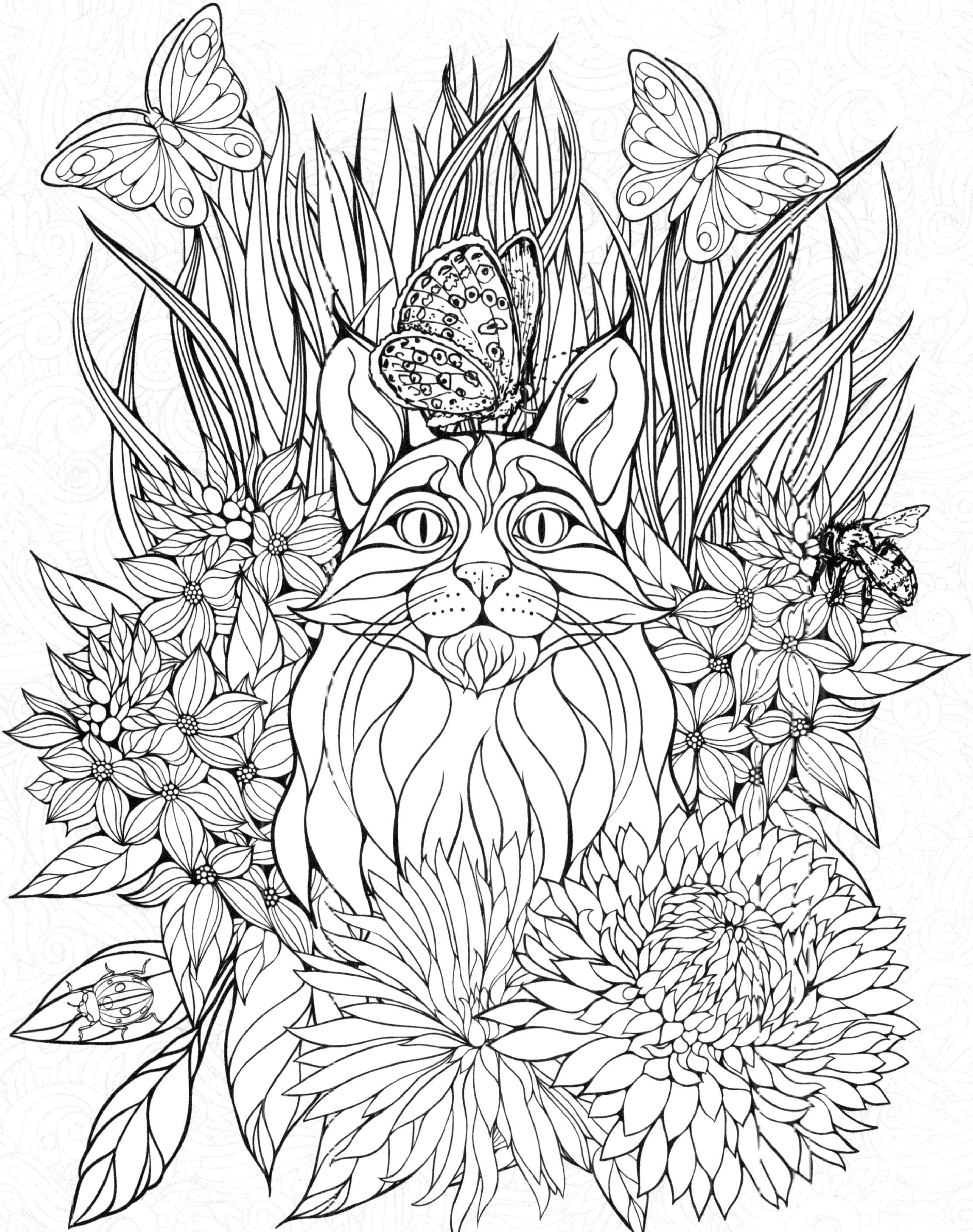

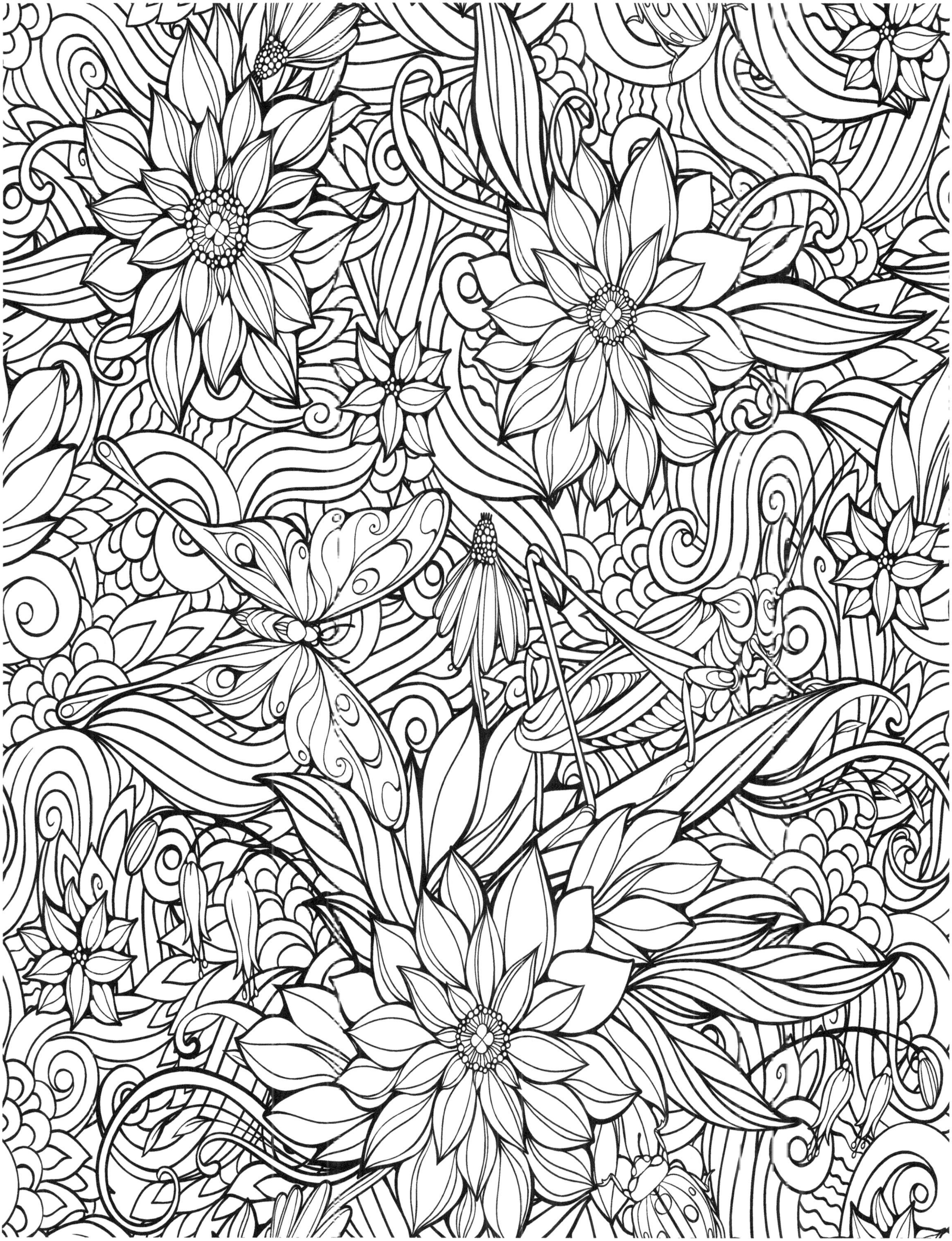

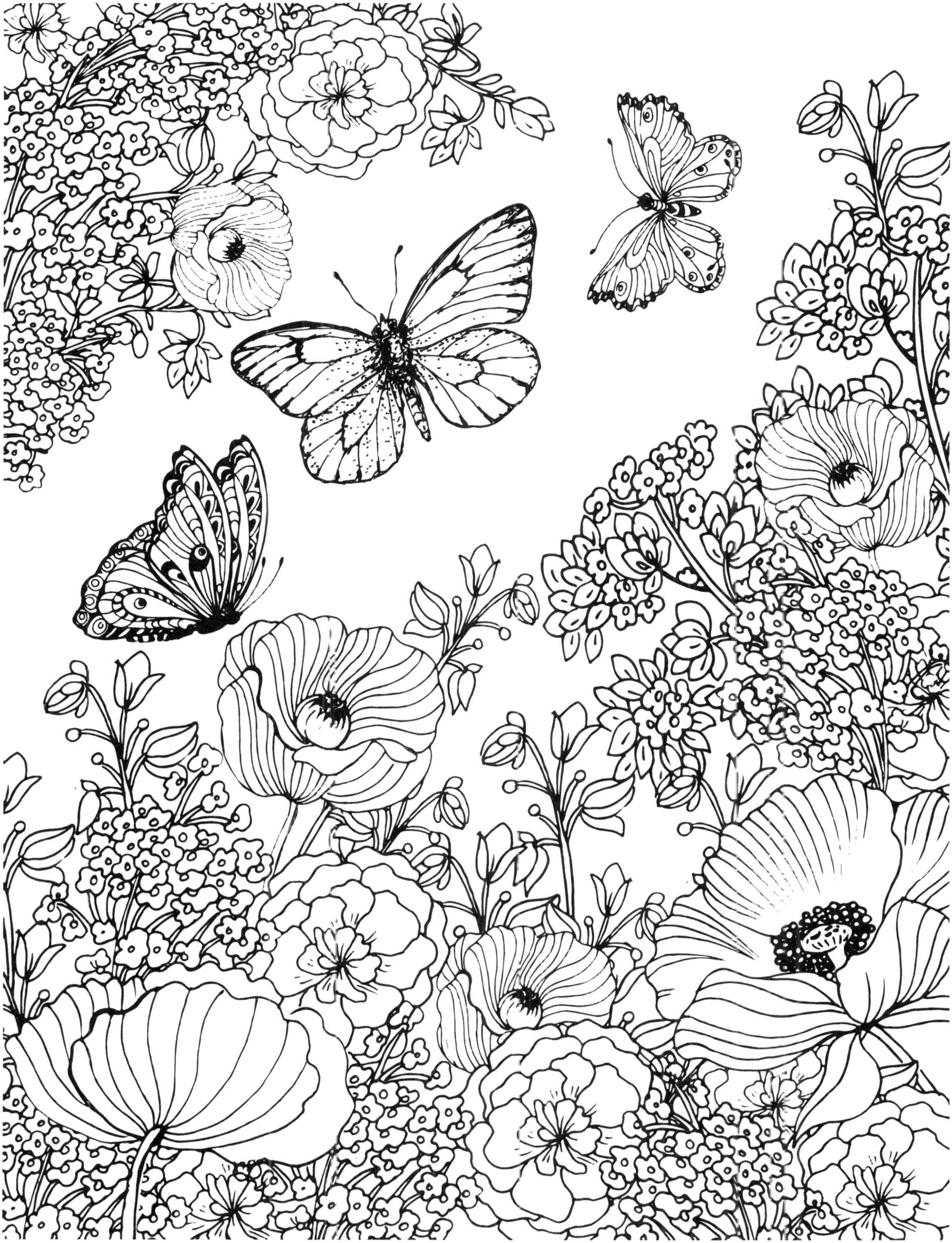

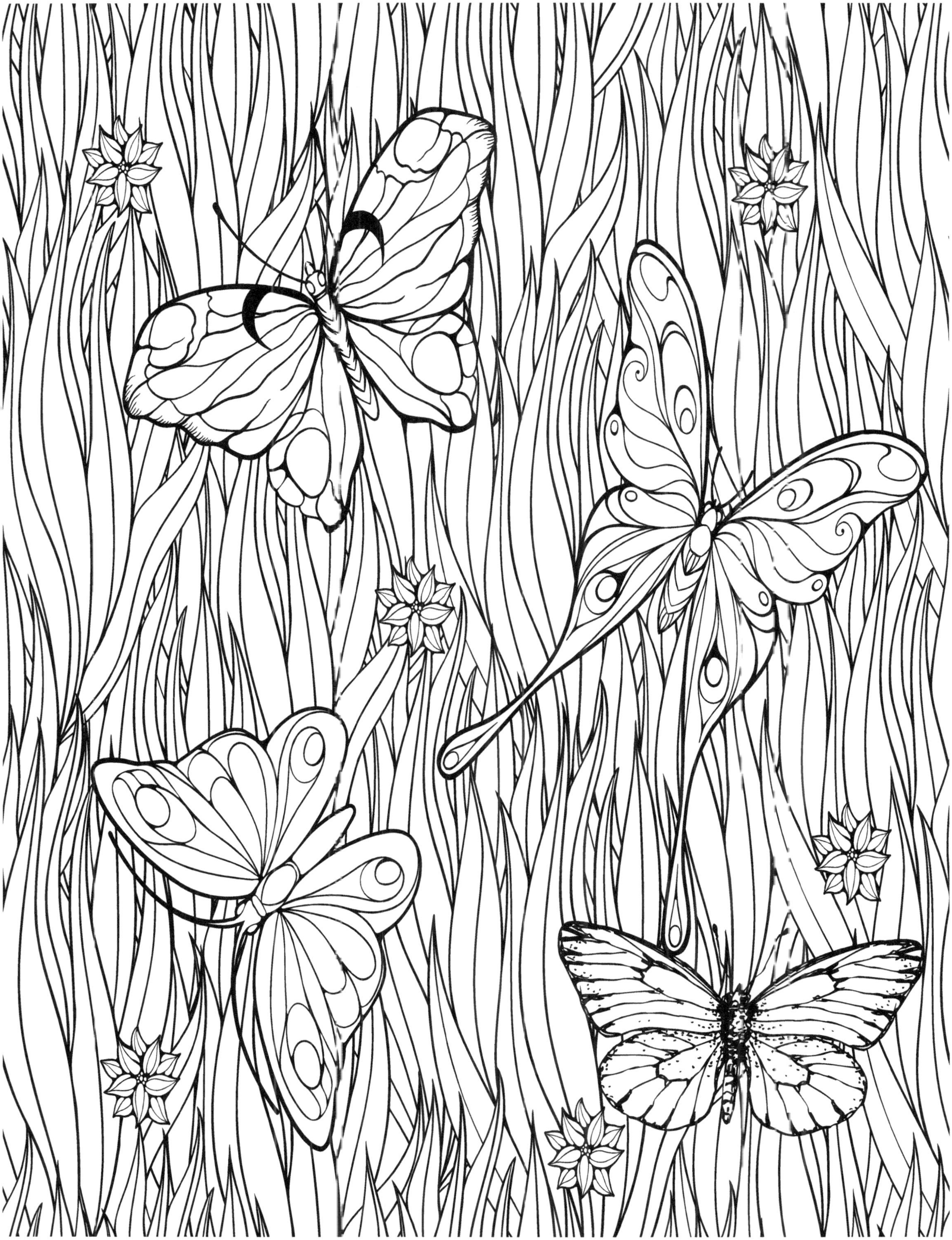

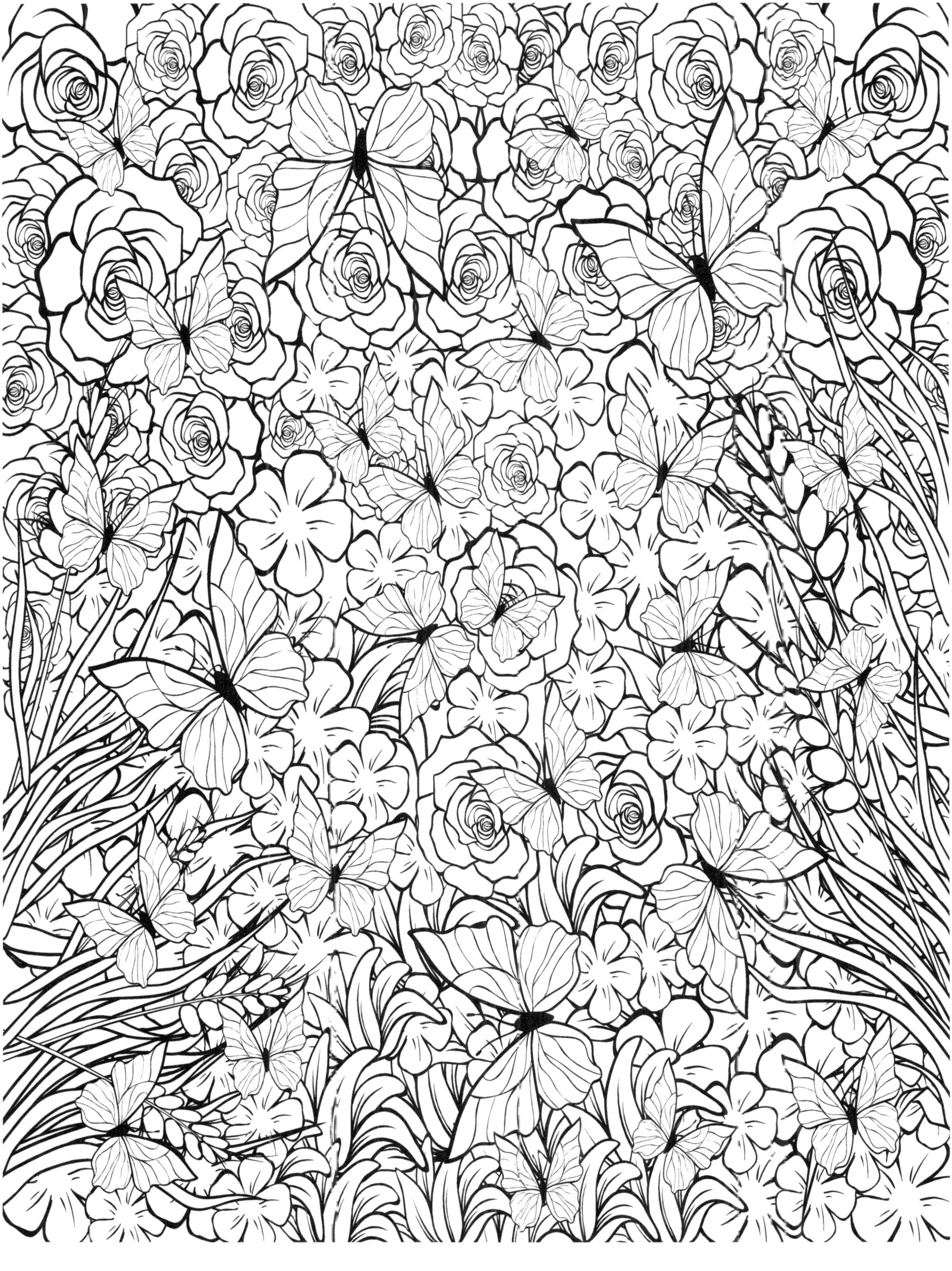

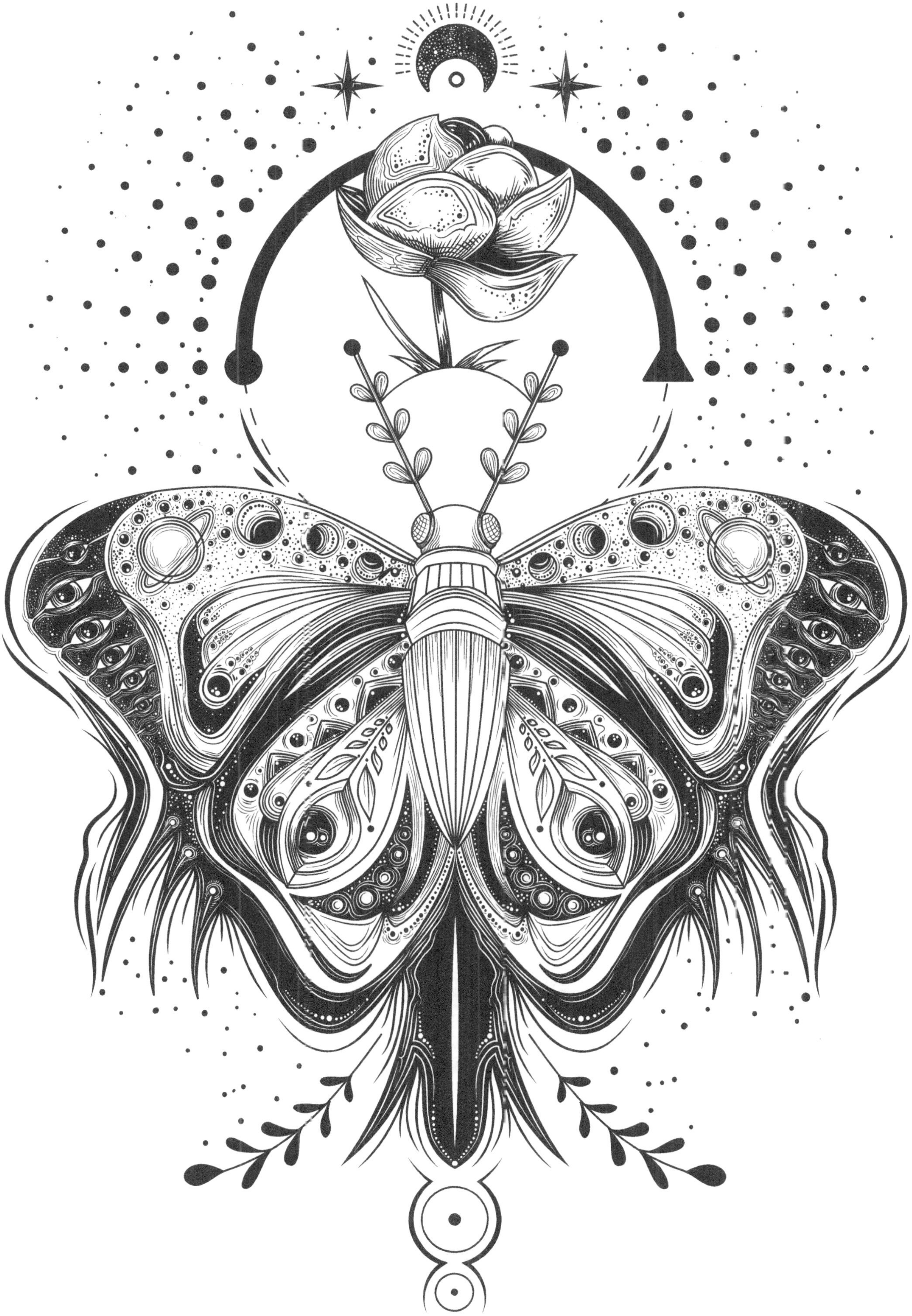

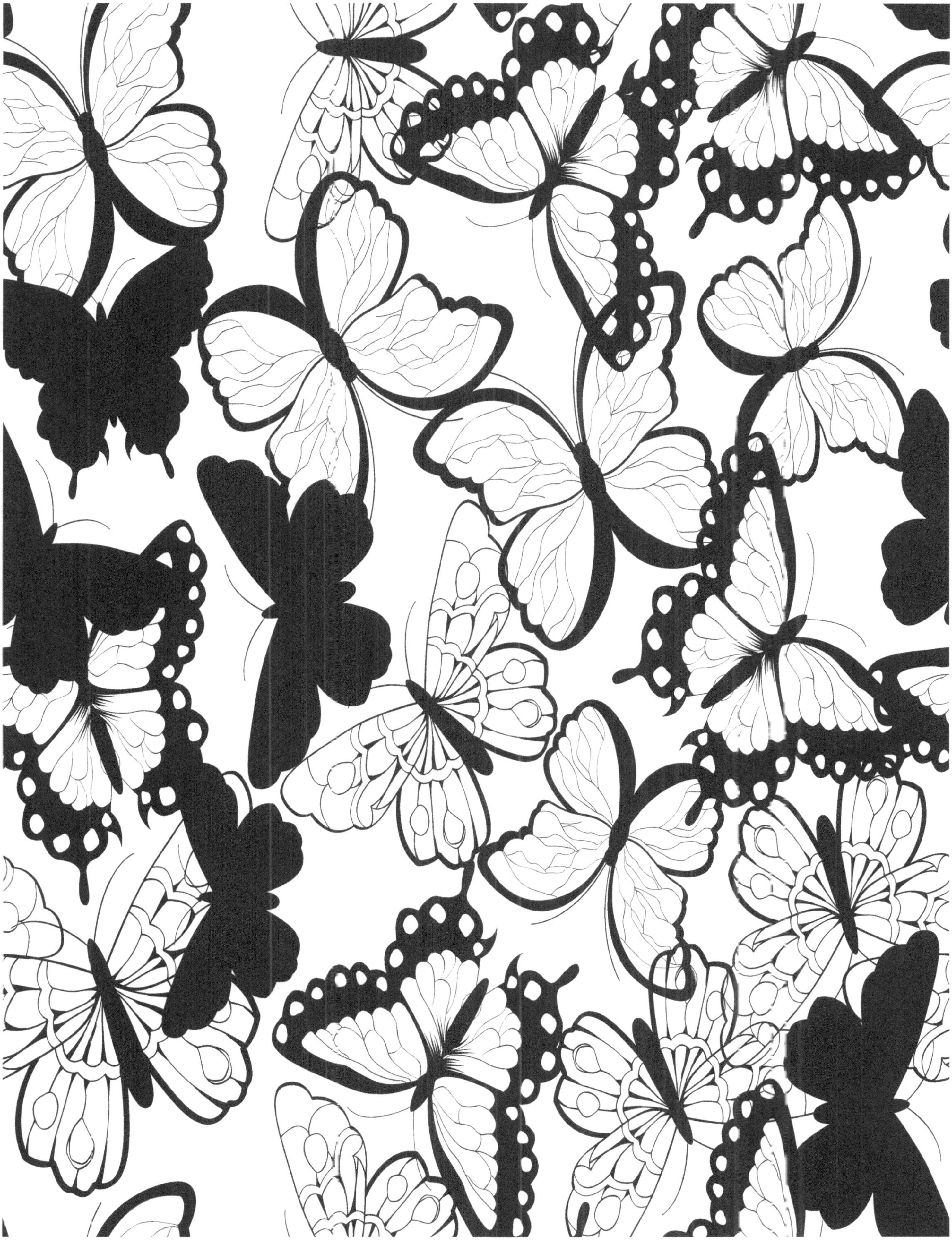

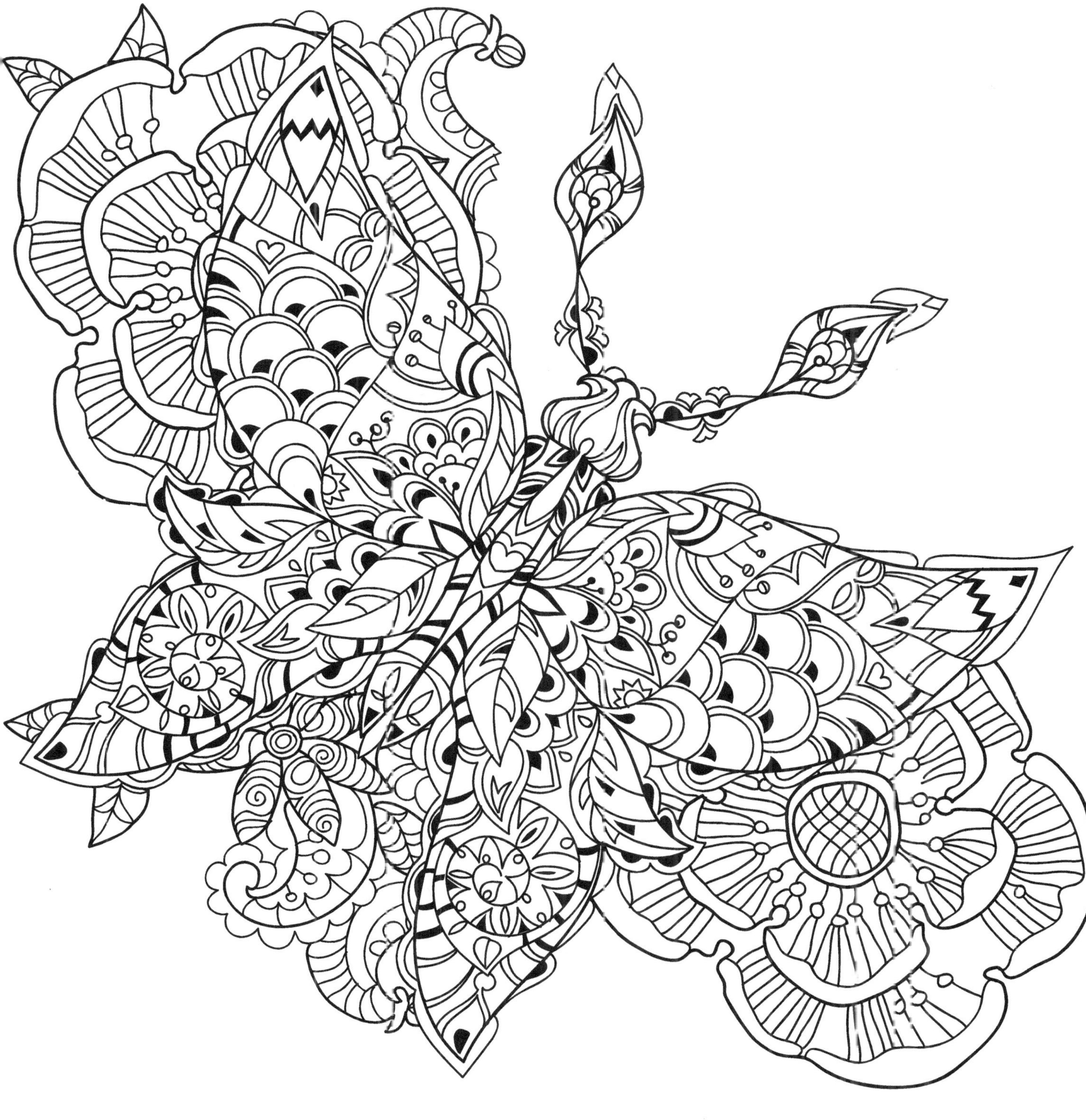

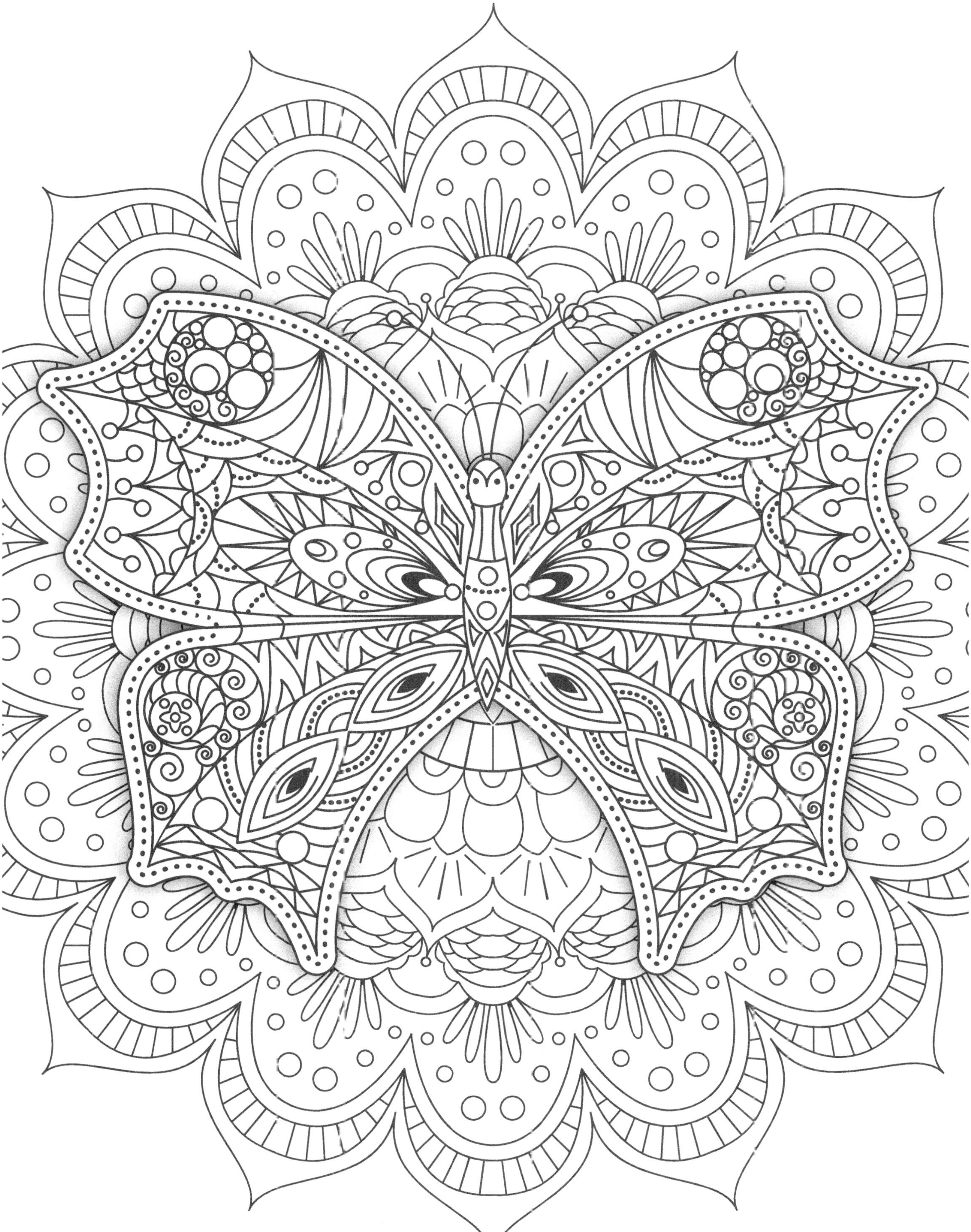

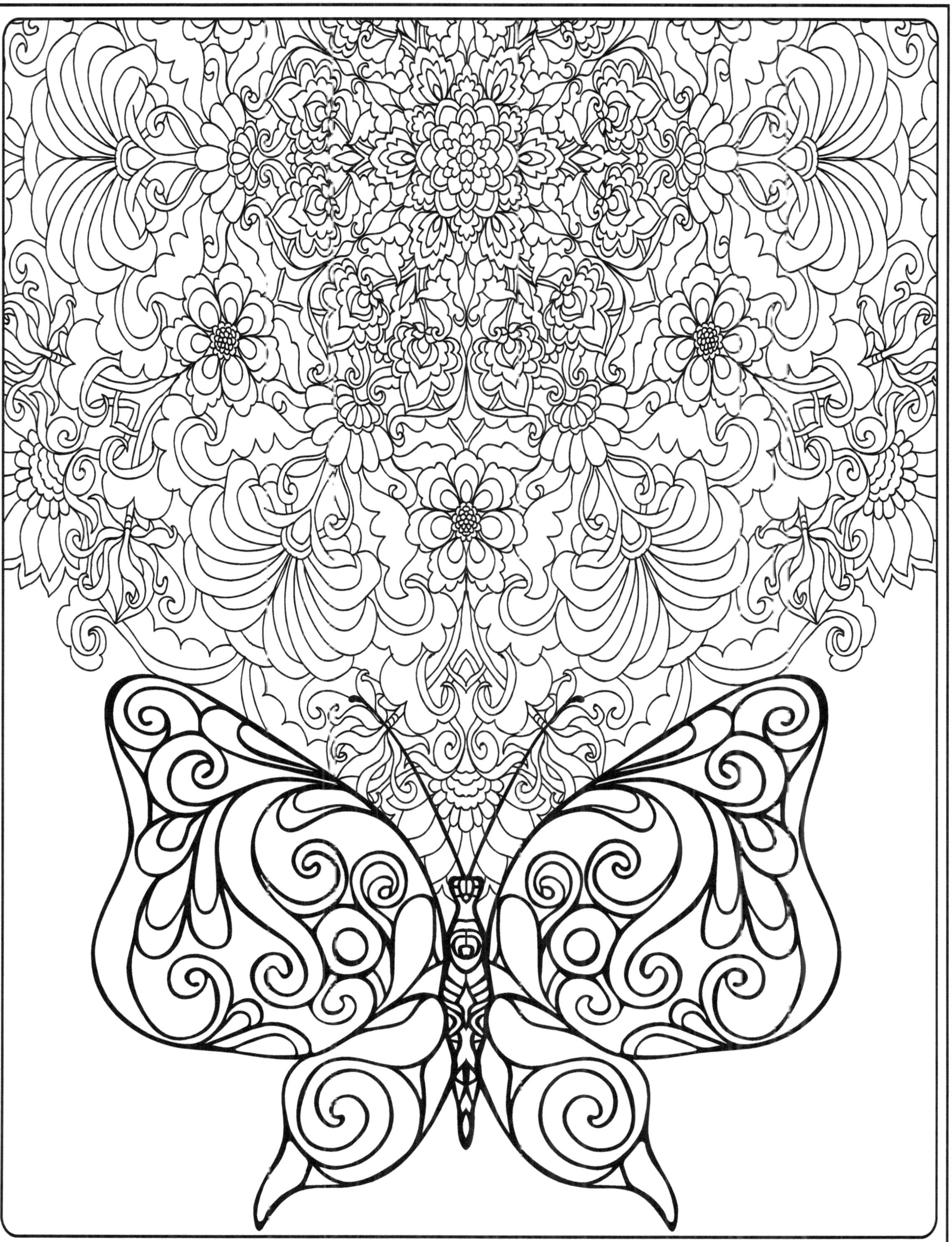

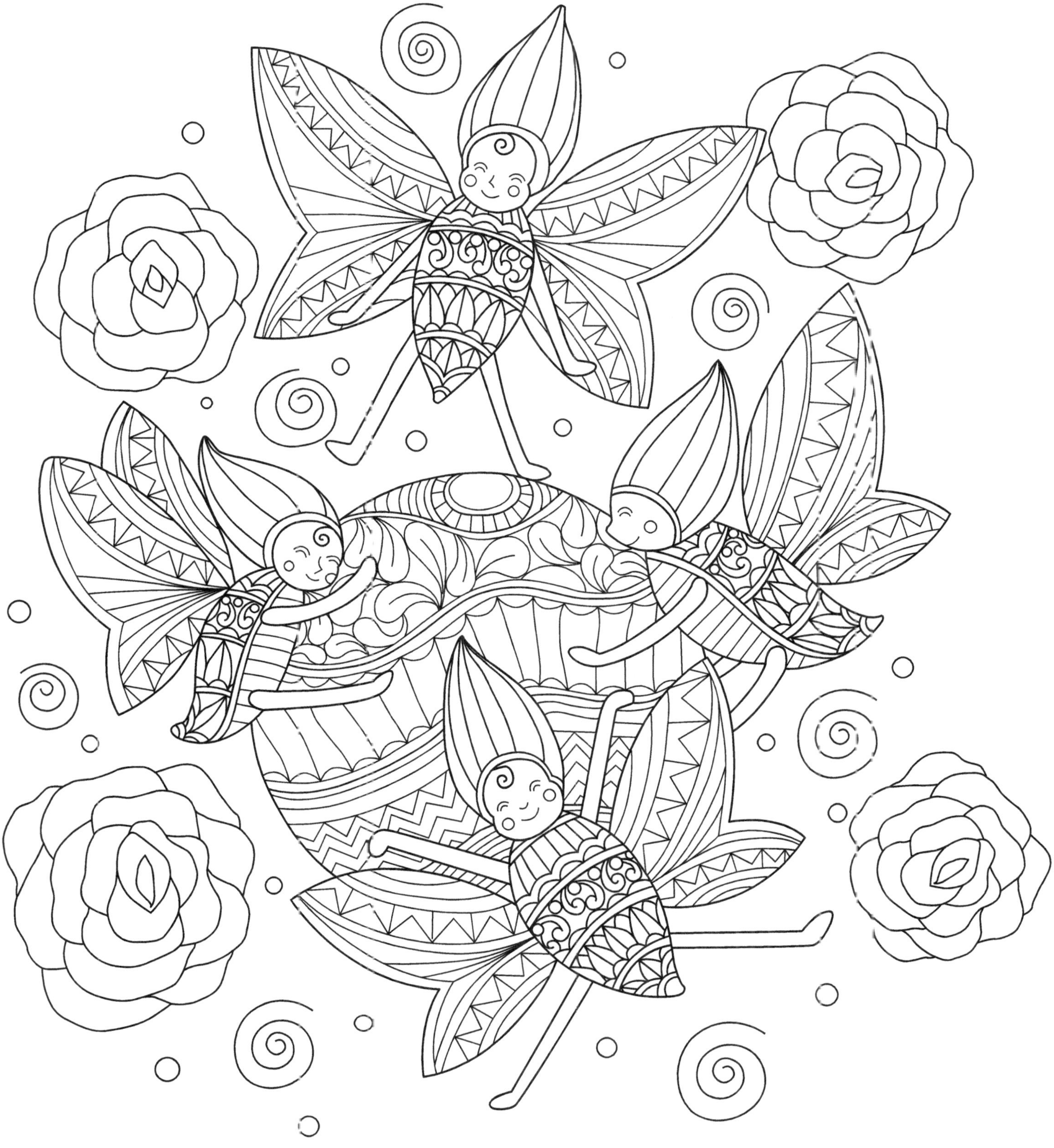

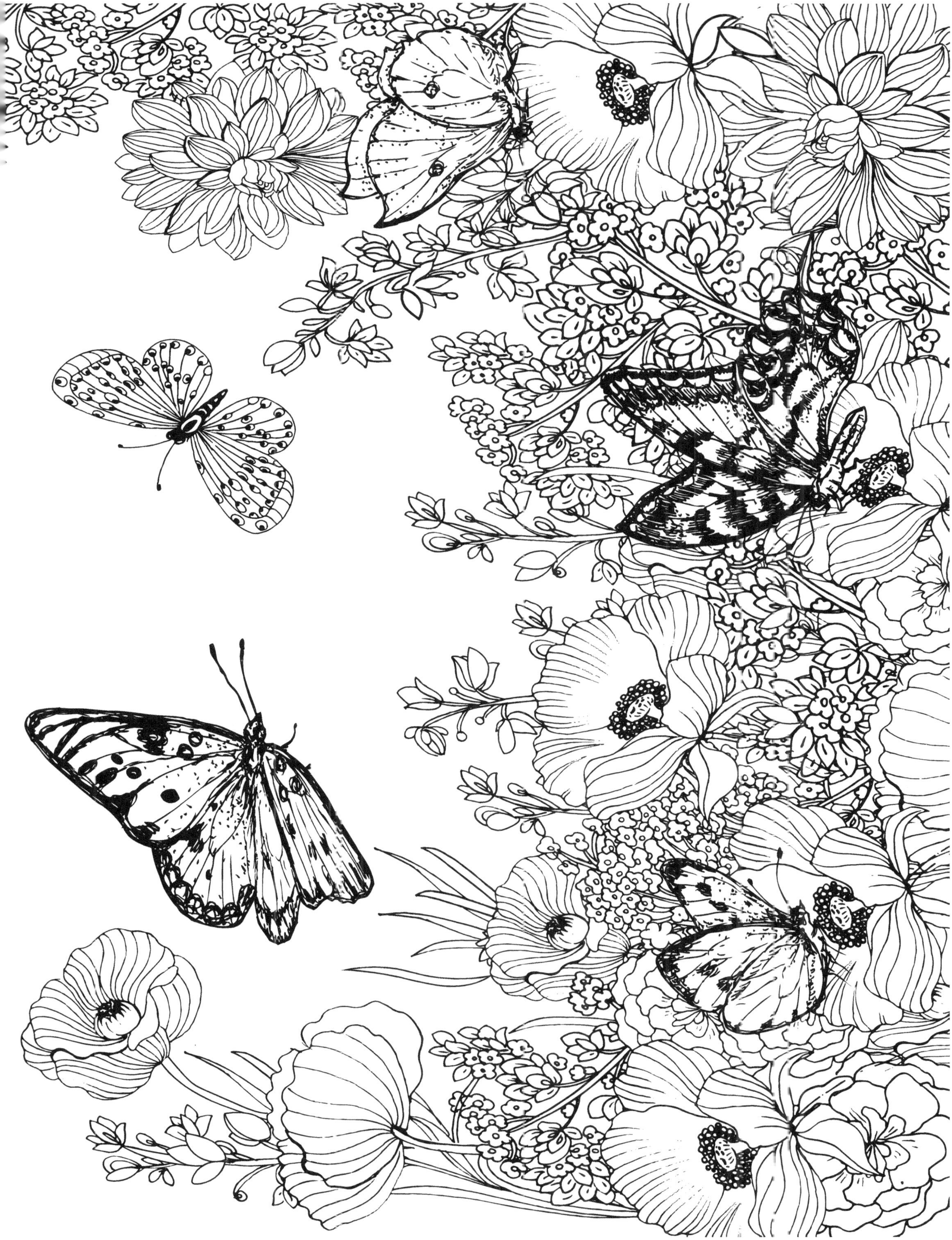

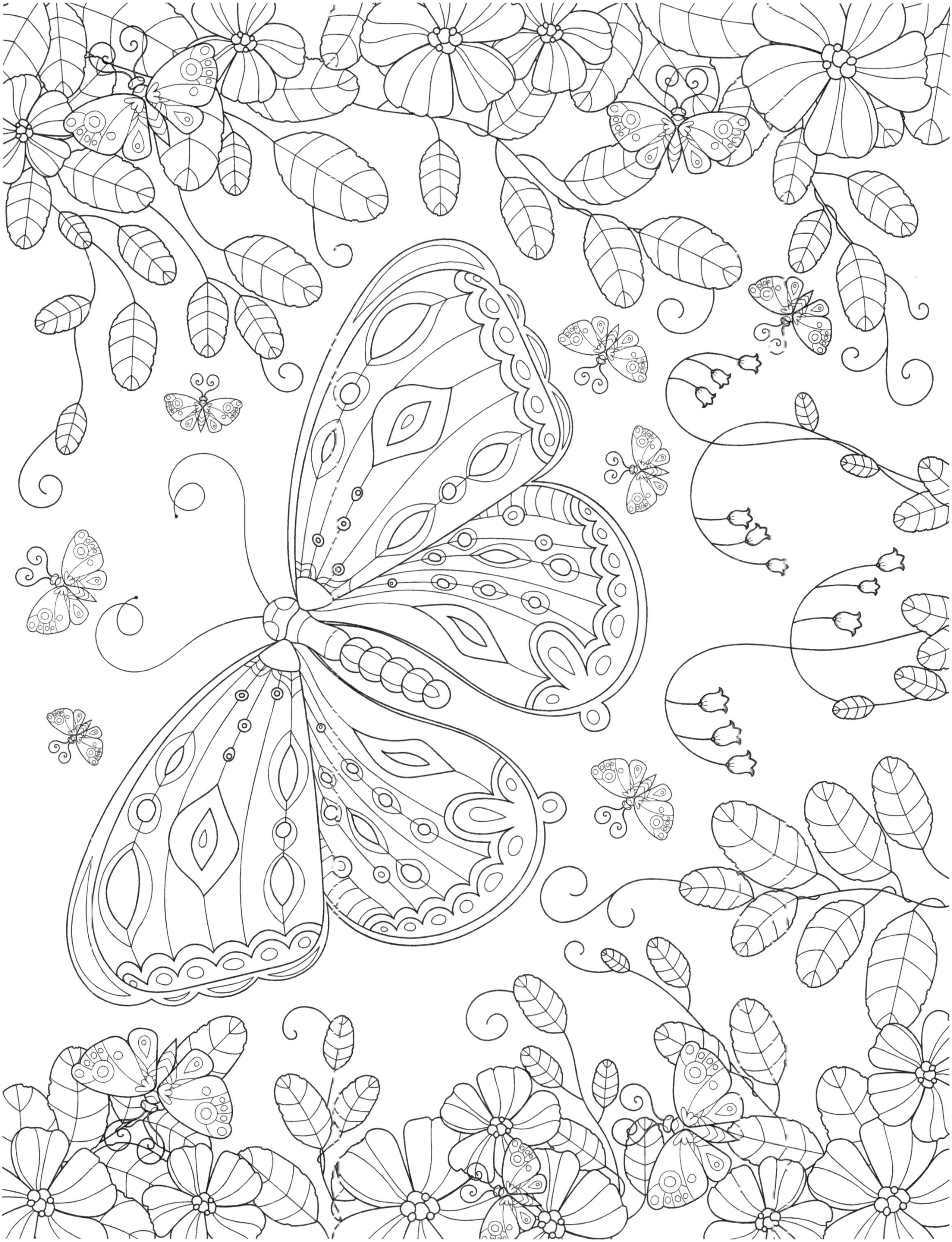

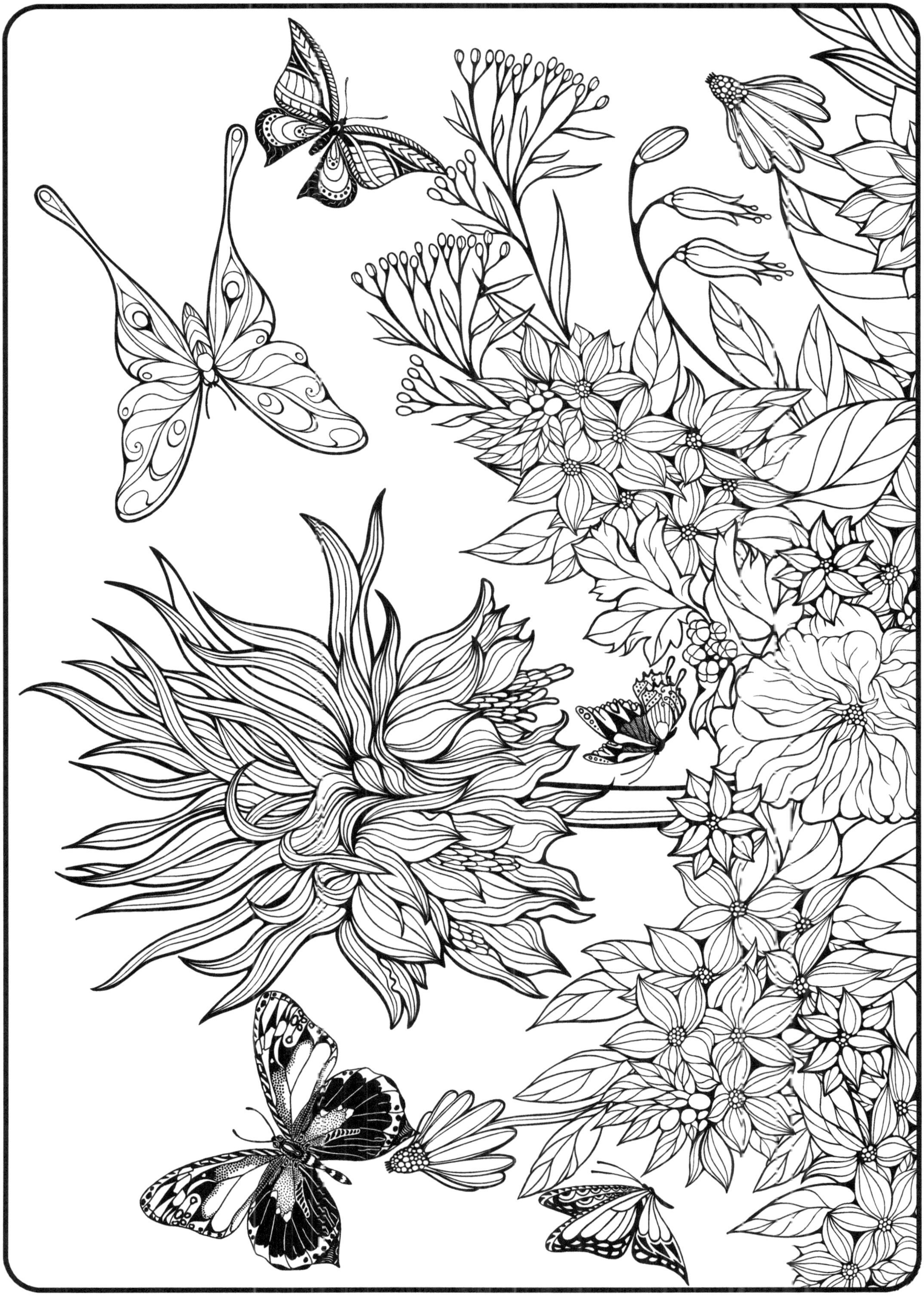

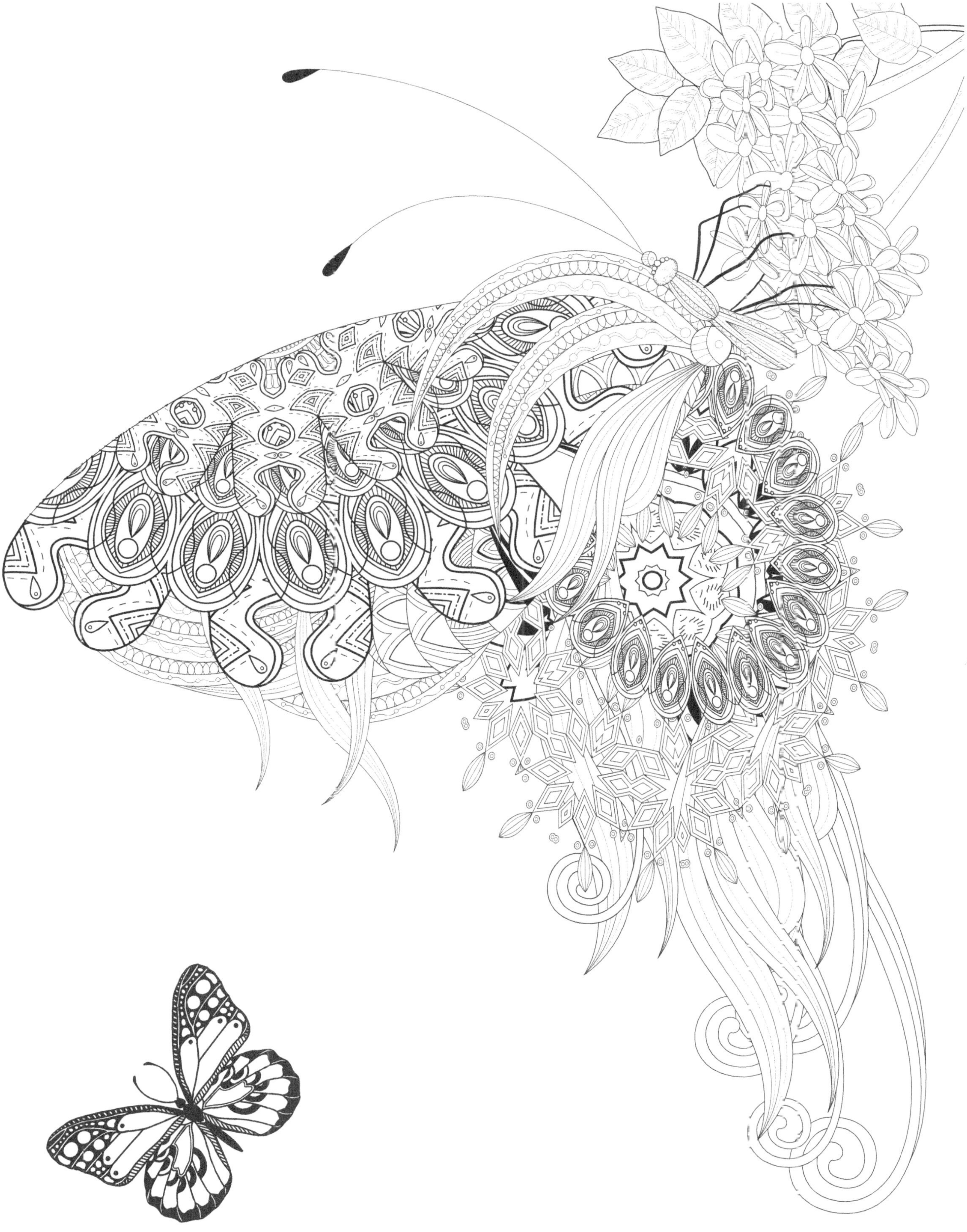

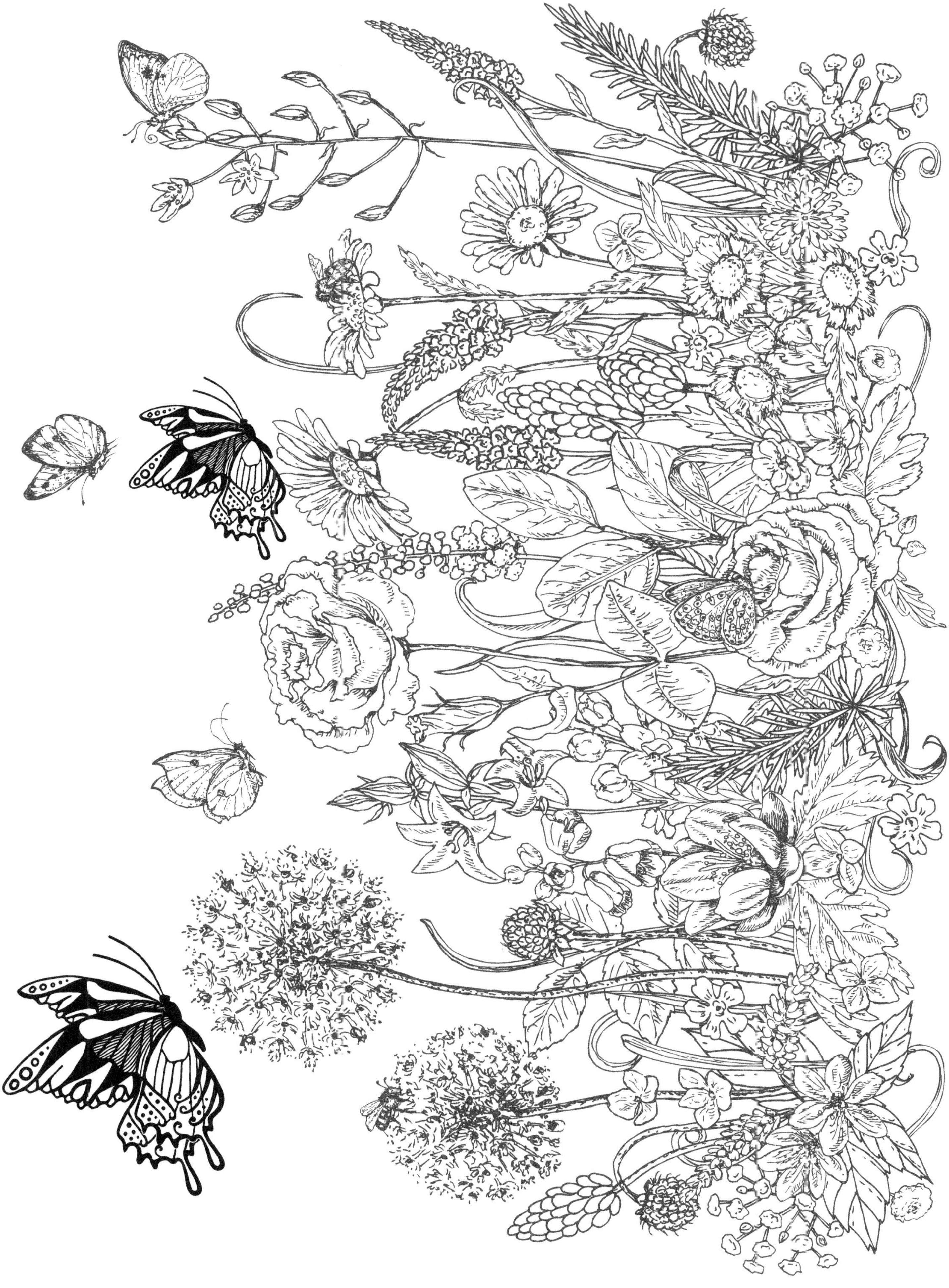

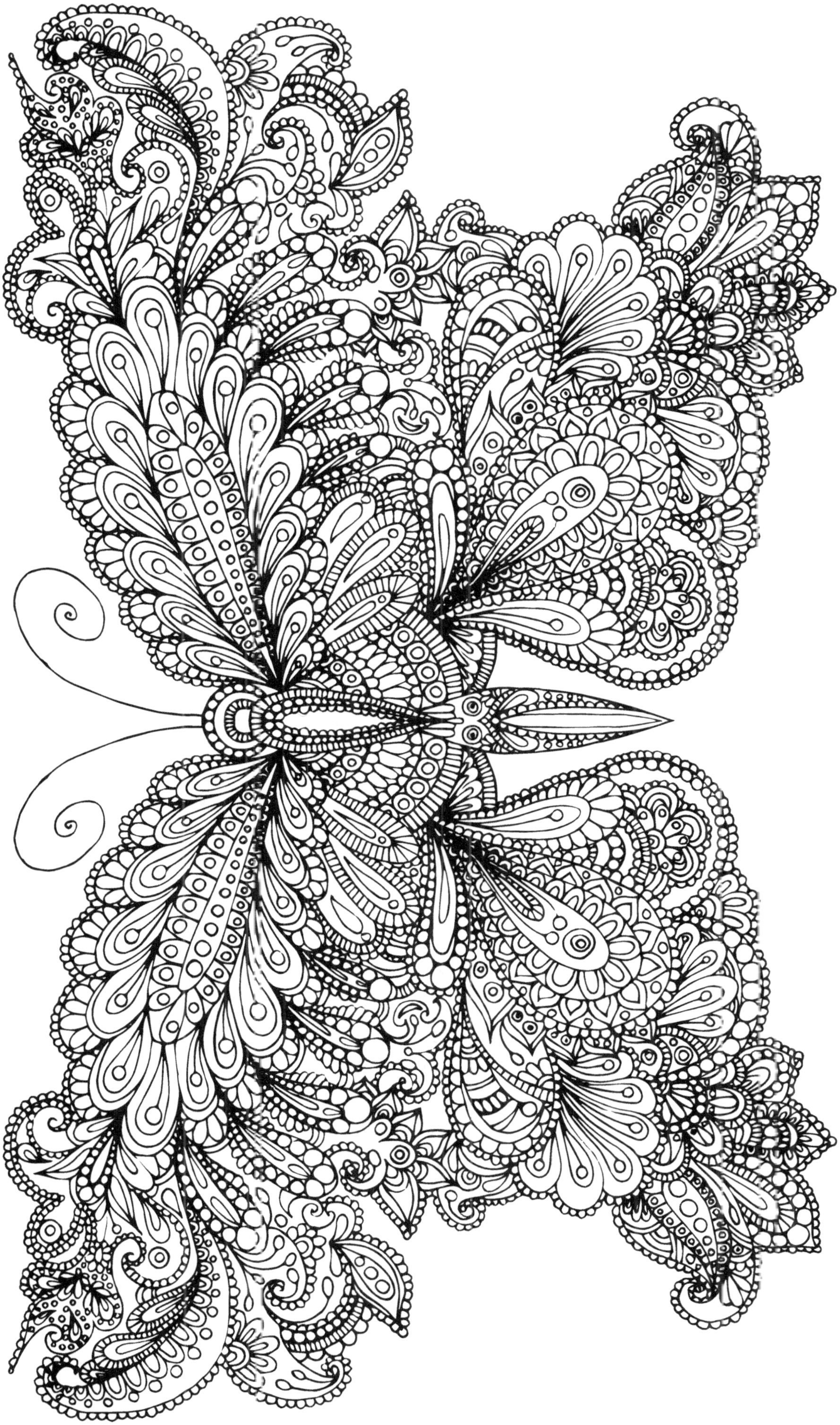

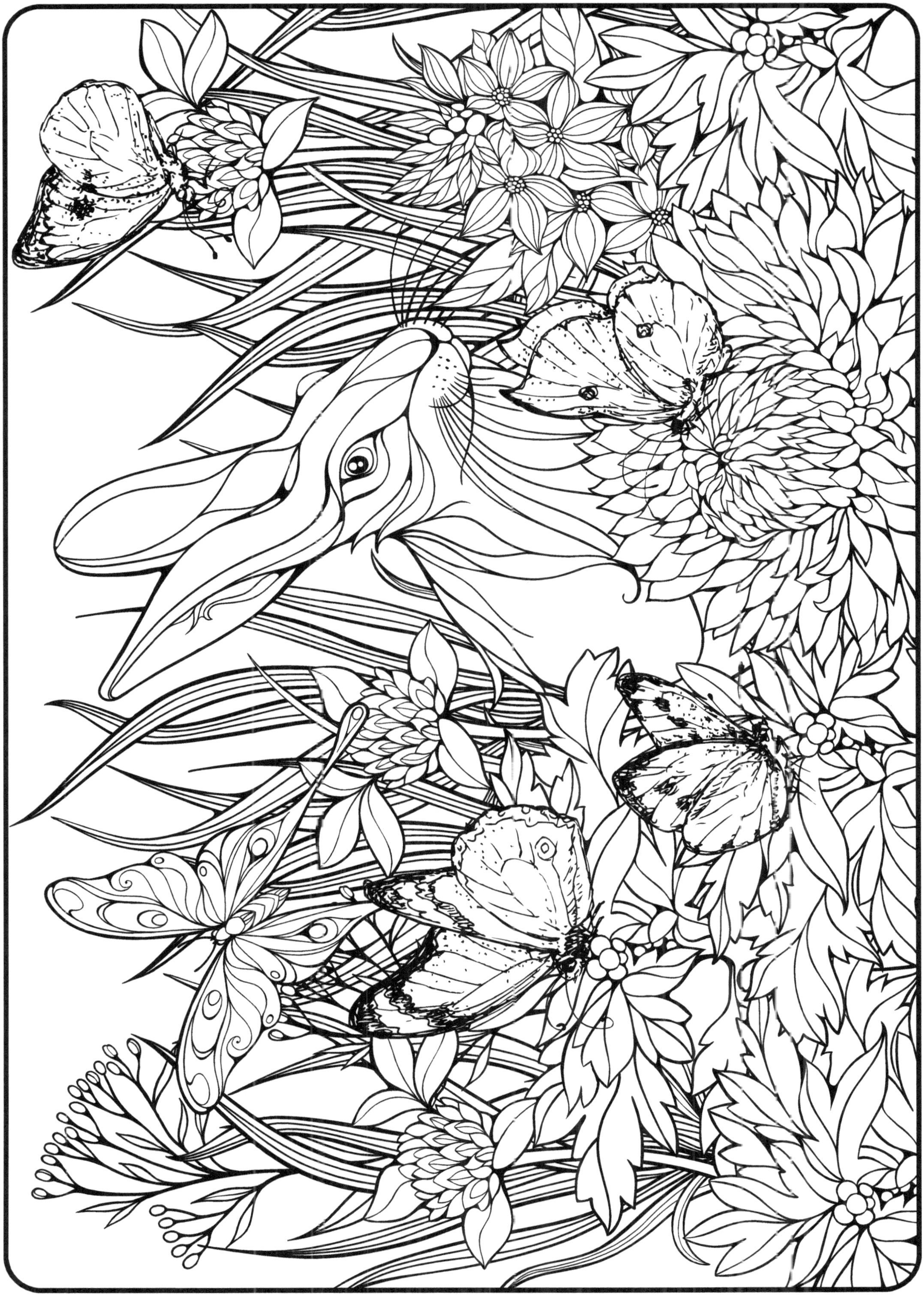

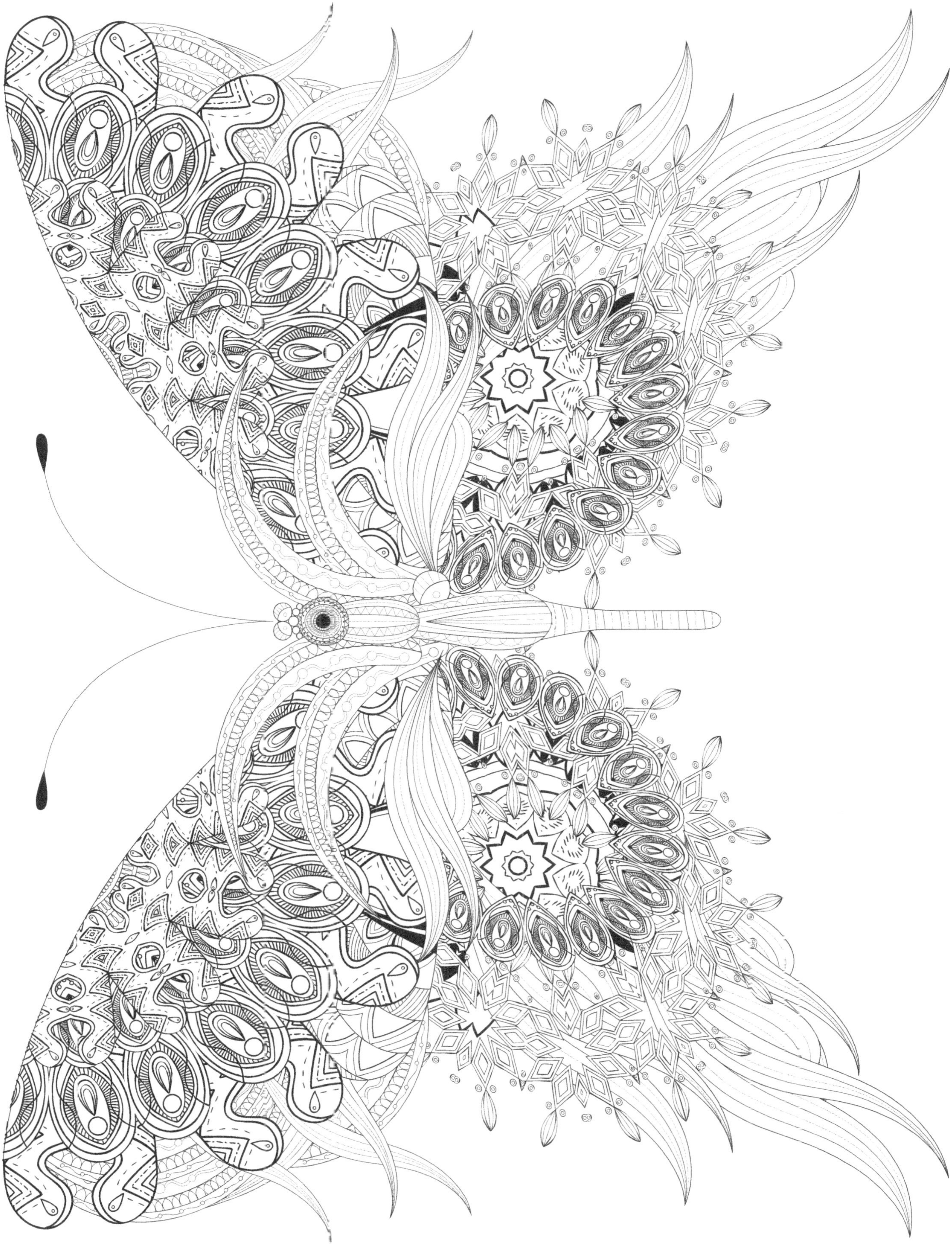

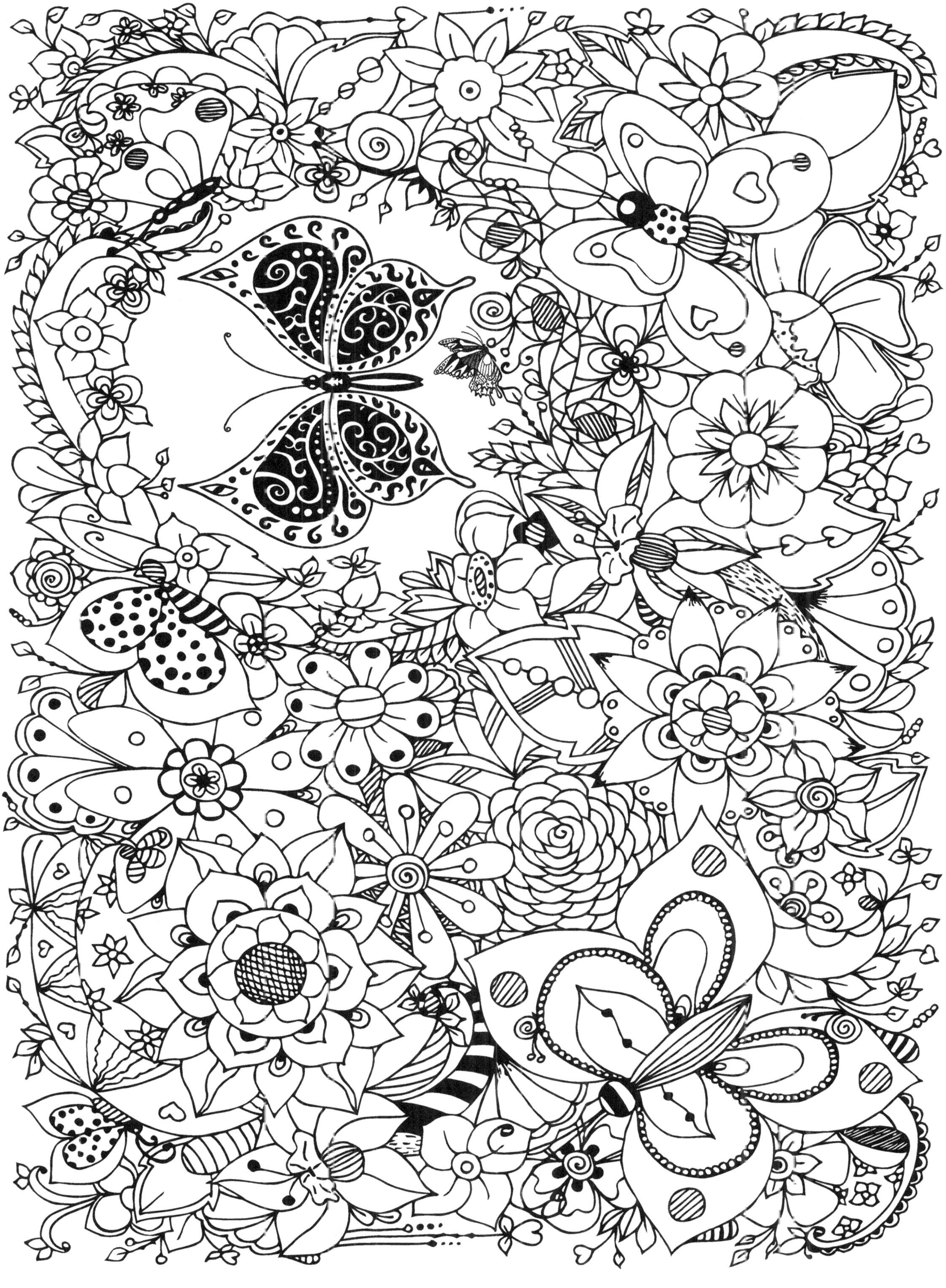

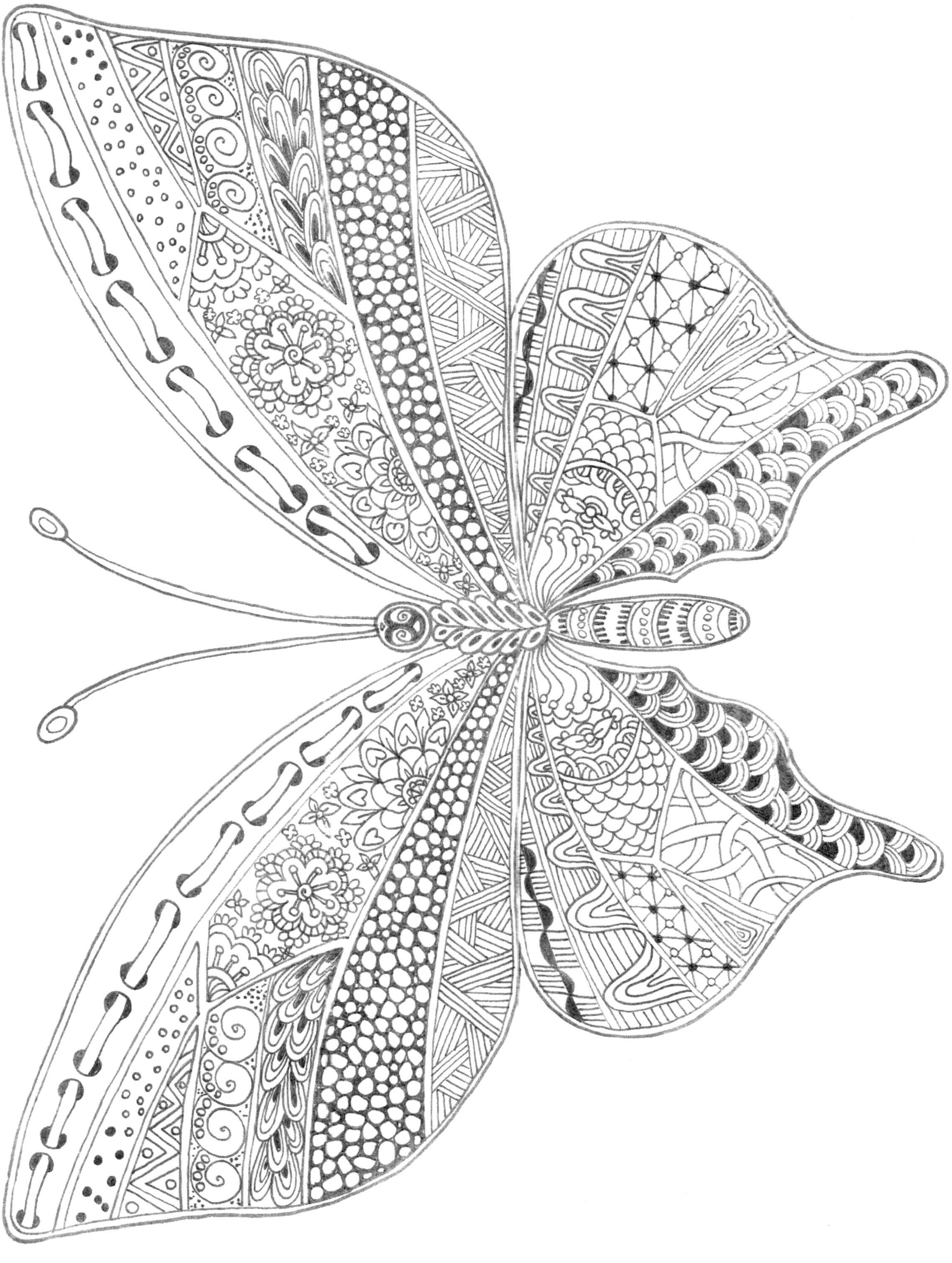

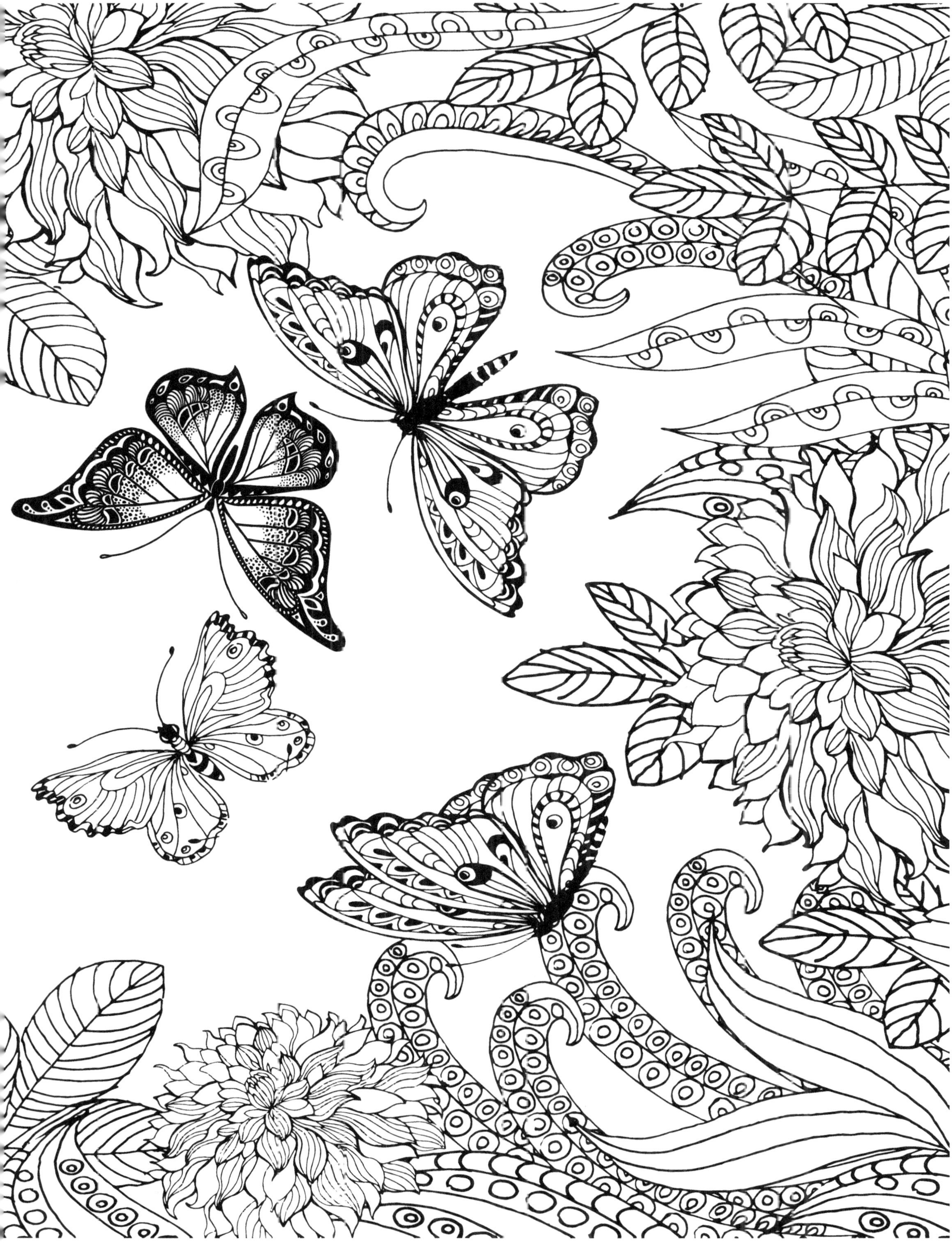

FREE BUTTERFLY COLORING PAGES

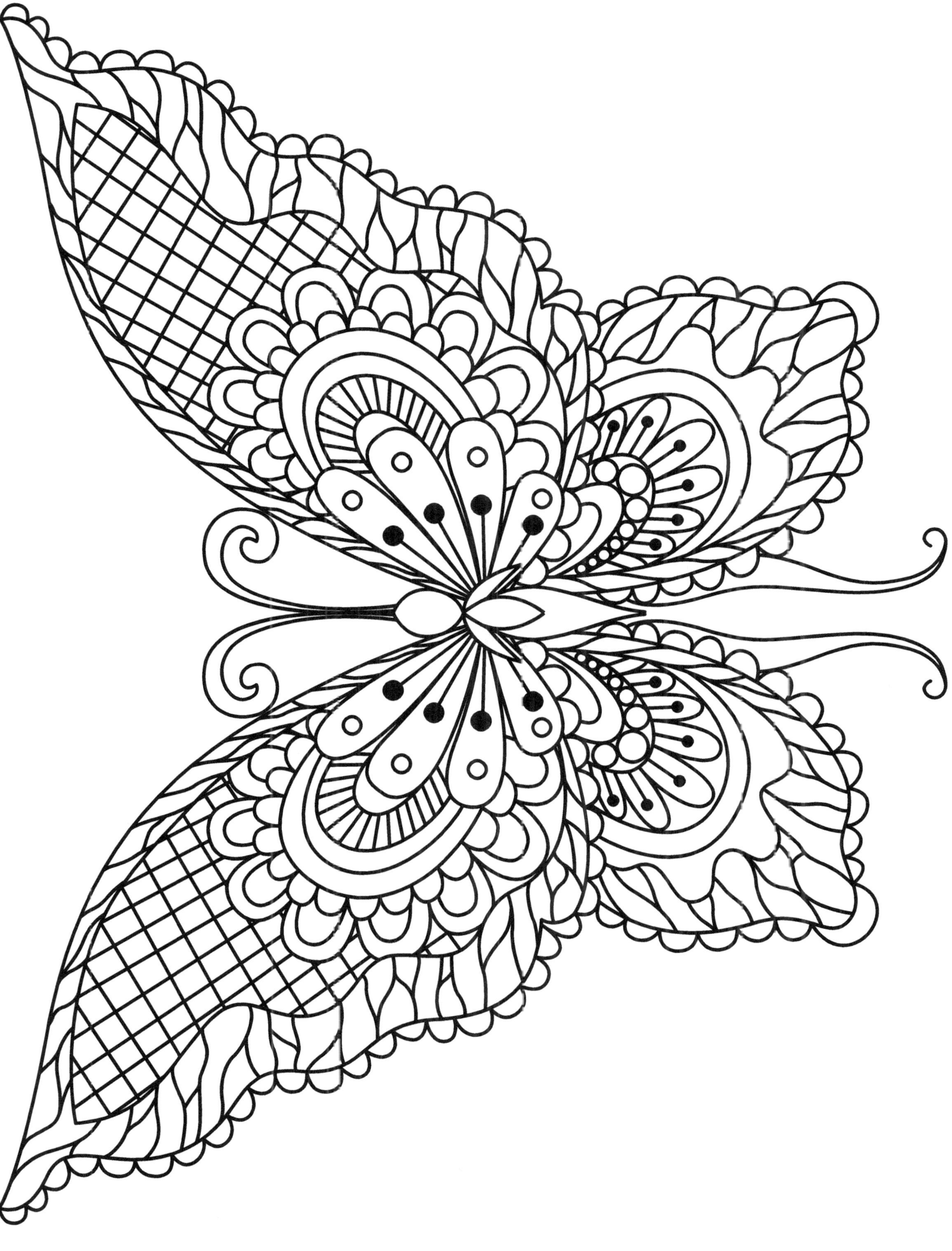

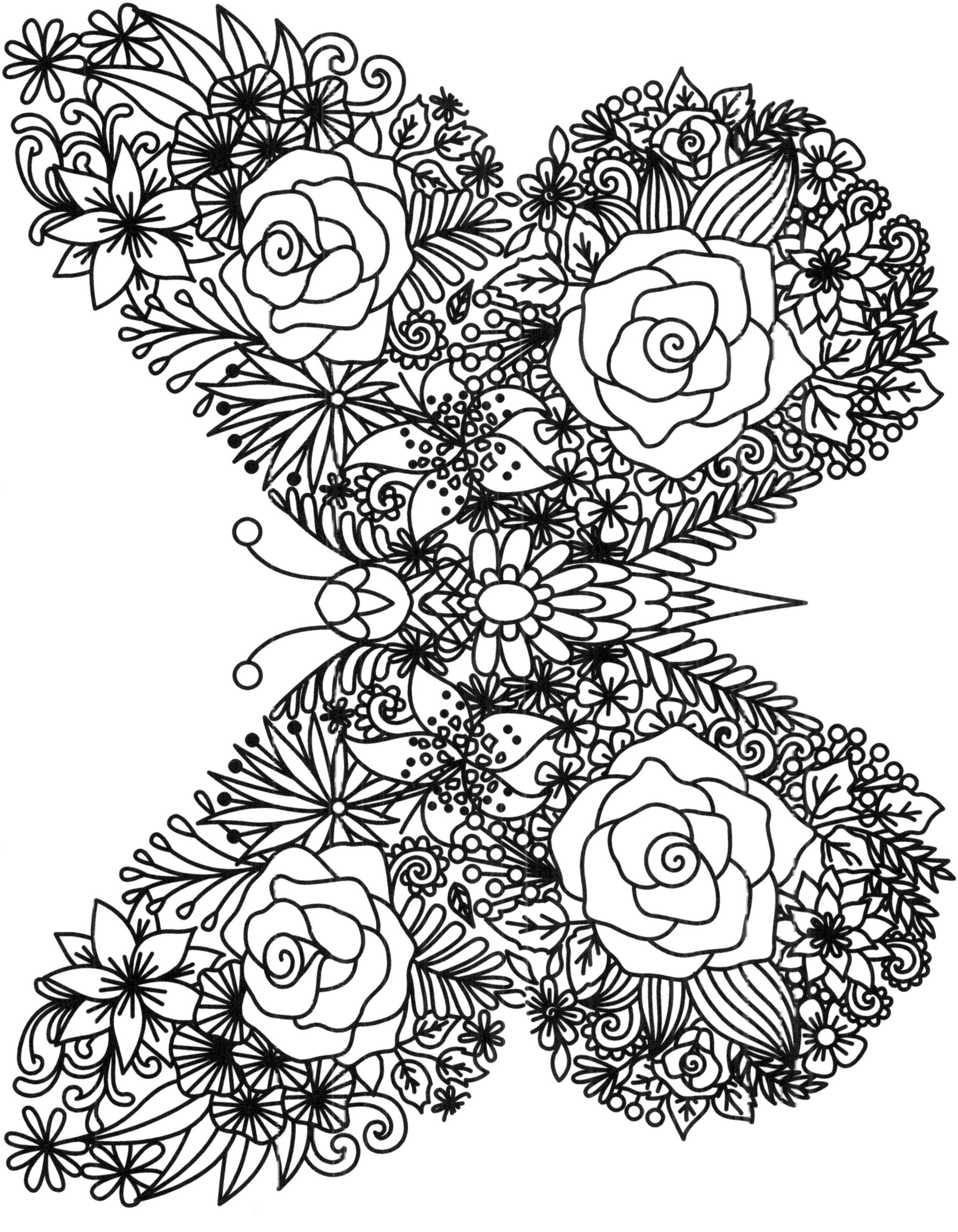

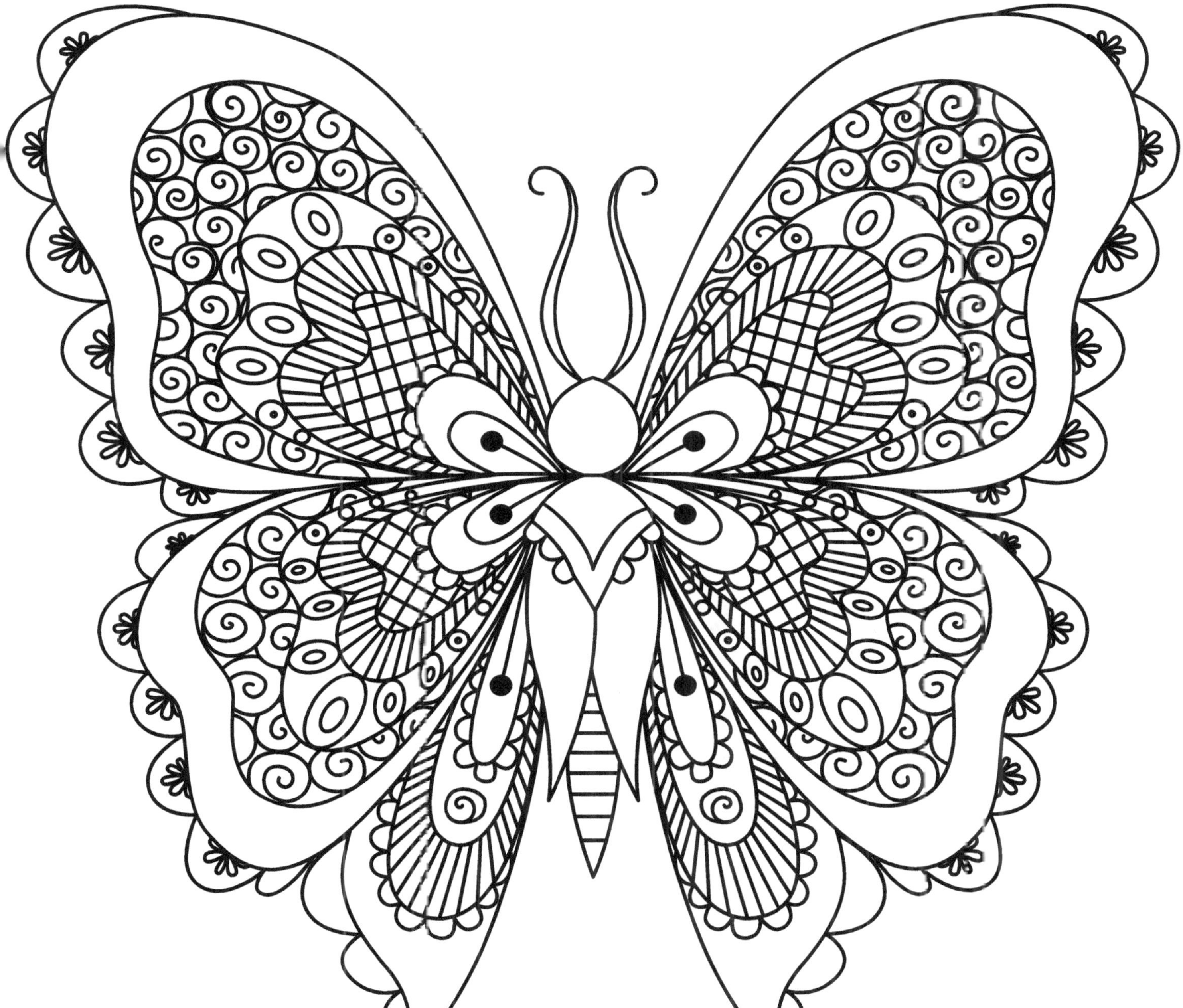

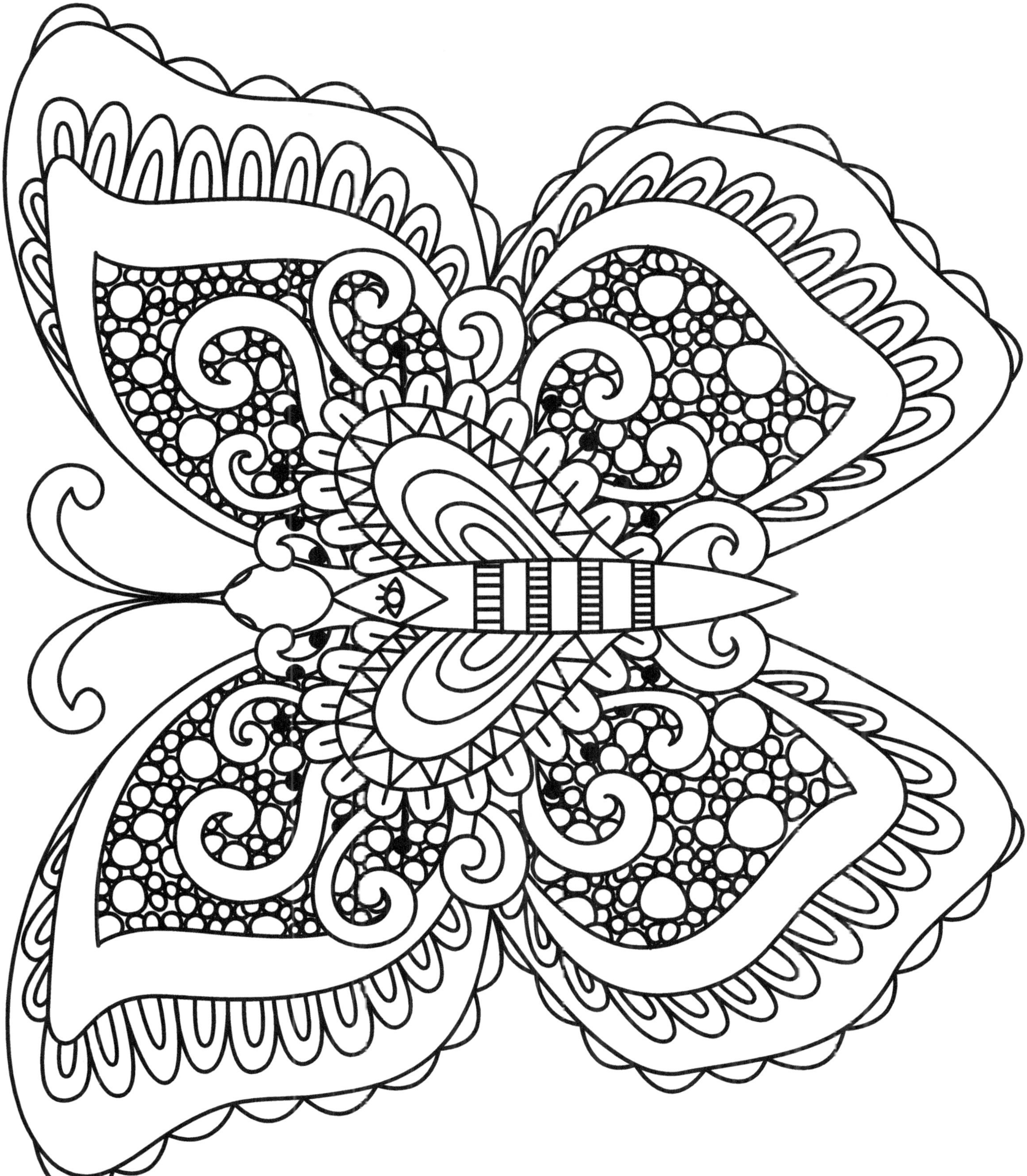

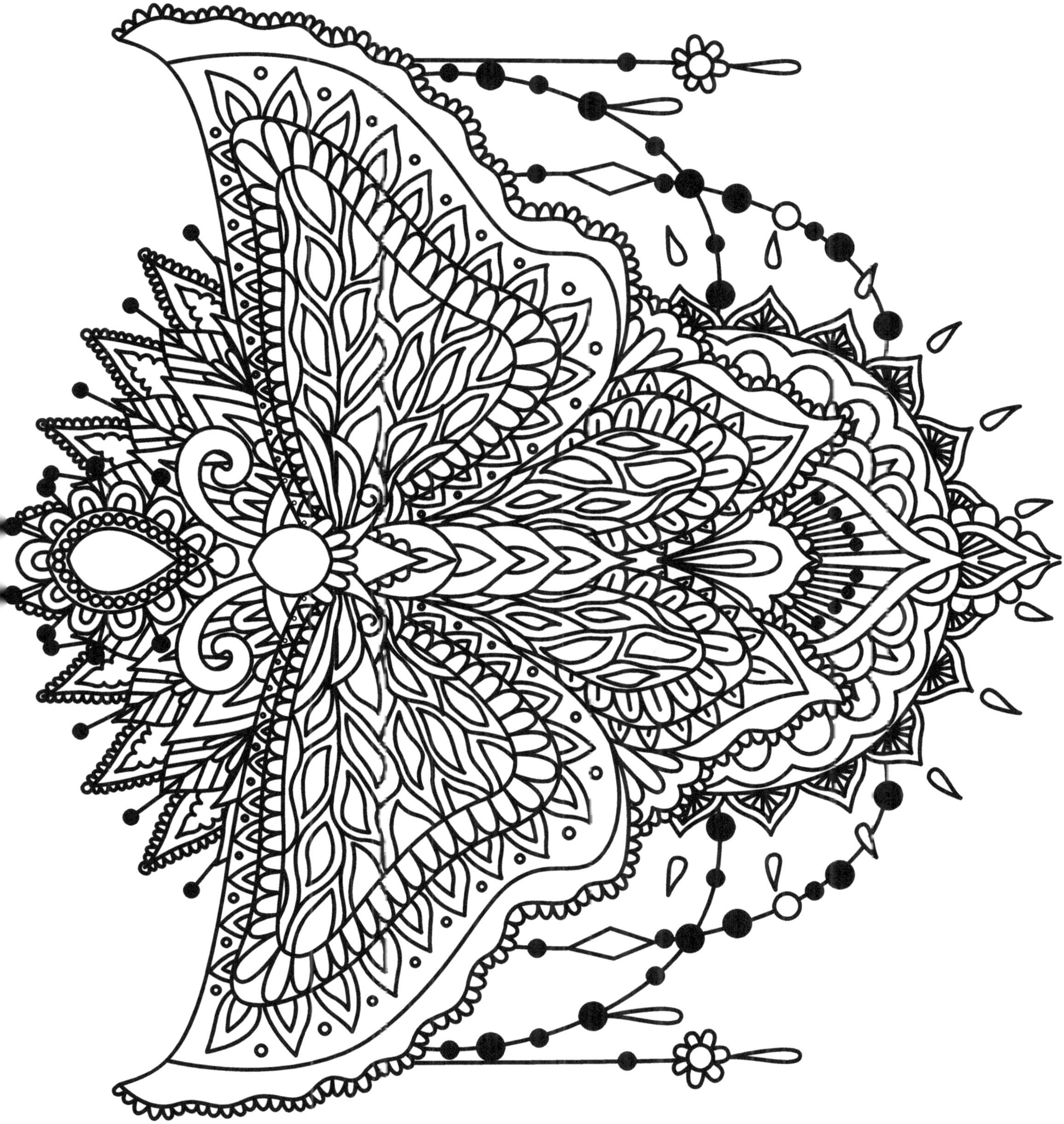

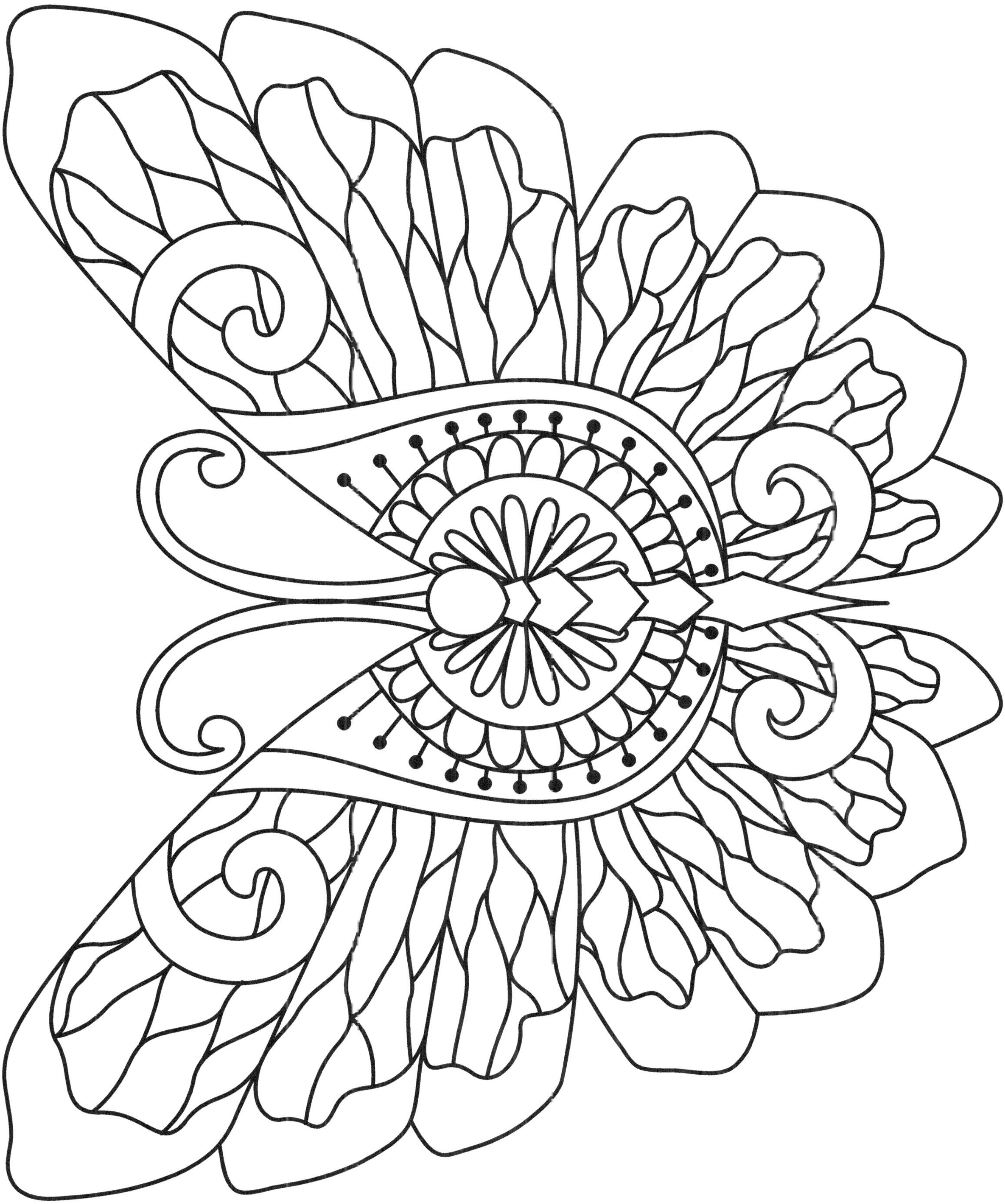

www.ingramcontent.com/pod-product-compliance
Lightning Source LLC
Chambersburg PA
CBHW062332220526
45469CB00008B/2686
9781727088816